"*Don't Run from the Figh* improve—their own psy between science and stor intuitions, reactions, and ...... an inspiring leader who makes his lessons relatable by sharing his struggles and eventual successes! I highly recommend this book!"

—Chris Cooper
Founder, Two-Brain Business

"This book is a *gift*. The story and tactical format are brilliantly woven together to give us real insight and strategy to overcome our own roadblocks. This *is* the book men (and their wives) of all ages need to read...*now!*

"*Don't Run from the Fight* hits all the major topics men quietly battle every day. Eric Freedom does an amazing job sharing riveting personal stories and weaving them into lessons for anyone. This book dances wonderfully from story to problem to laying out a blueprint for success in some of the most important issues men battle, such as anger, identity, isolation, purpose, emotional mastery, and more. Not often do I find a book that is as entertaining, relevant, and strategic as *Don't Run from the Fight*."

—Scott Rammage
Husband and Father
Host of the Brotherhood of Fatherhood Podcast

"*Don't Run from the Fight* is a thoughtful and actionable guide for men rooted in strength, wisdom, and self-compassion. Through reflections on his experiences, Eric Freedom provides a personal roadmap from tough, painful circumstances to courageous, perseverant leadership. For men seeking to find or reclaim their purpose and power, this book shows the path from victim to victory."

—Bonnie J. Skinner MEd.,RP
Registered Psychotherapist
Executive Mental Fitness Coach
CEO, Level Up Mental Fitness

"Wow! This book hits home. While it's written with young men in mind, this is a great resource for anyone embracing their hero's journey. Eric lays out a framework built on self-reflection, ownership, and action to assist you in becoming the version of yourself you've aspired to be. For those who find themselves burned out and uninspired, the 'Freedom Framework' will help you dust yourself off and get back to the fight."

—Jacob Saldana
Holistic Hustler
Multi-Location Gym Owner
Founder of Space B.A.R. Wellness, The Fit Bar Superfood Cafe, & Lifted Botanical Bar

"Plenty of books teach young men to be financially and entrepreneurially successful. But that's a one-legged or two-legged stool at best that still leaves you on the floor—disappointed and unfulfilled. You've heard the stories: multi-millionaires and billionaires on their fifth marriage, overweight or dealing with other health issues, and lacking healthy relationships. What kind of success is this? It's no wonder people give up.

"If you're willing to be honest with yourself, if you know life can be better, if you're looking to be your best self on *all* cylinders—spiritually, mentally, emotionally, relationally, and purposefully—immerse yourself into this book. Take action on its principles. Refer back to it often. Bonus points if you share this with others so they can be free, purpose-driven, and wholly successful too.

"You can sense from the pages that Eric is not interested in feel-good, superficial, empty, and short-lived strategies. He goes deep into your soul, where unanswered questions, true potential, and the root of our problems are hidden. He does so by sharing his relatable journey of youth, loss (broke my heart), growing up too fast, confusion, discouragement, and unanswered questions. Why? So that you know you're not alone and can do it.

"*Don't Run from the Fight* is the book I wish I had while growing up, especially when Eric talks about mindset. As a young entrepreneur, Asian-American, once divorced husband, and dad, this book could have saved me from many of the toxic stories I've told myself.

"Even though the best time to have this guide was at the start of my journey, the second best time is *now*. I'm excited to recapture my joy and live purposefully. Thank you for this labor of love, this display of courage and generosity, and this mission of helping others like you and me. Mission accomplished."

—Paul T Tran
Serial Entrepreneur
Advisor, Speaker, Investor
Writer of *Eff Around & Find Out*
YouTube & Podcast Host of Unfocused Show

"Looking for purpose, meaning, and clarity? Eric Freedom is candid and direct in his book, *Don't Run from the Fight*, with tough yet valuable insights. This book is a fresh take on 'no pain, no gain'—no holds barred. The five growth strategies of Eric's 'Freedom Framework' are akin to a training regimen that is rigorous yet rewarding, particularly for the young man determined to grasp who he is, connect to what matters most, and bring to light who he's destined to be."

—Chris Chu
Retired Principal
Educator, Coach, Husband, and Father

"Eric is a seminal voice needed today for men of all generations. *Don't Run from the Fight* models integrity and God-given convictions worth pursuing. Eric's vulnerability will lend you the courage to experience breakthroughs in your journey of failure, self-doubt, and immobility. Finally, there is a path to freedom when you look in the mirror and decide you are worth the fight."

—Morris Li
Husband, Father, Home Educator
Leadership Coach & Chick-fil-A Owner/Operator

"*Don't Run from the Fight* is a great book for all to read, especially in a world that desperately needs leaders. Eric's raw and inspiring story of overcoming tremendous odds to create a life of purpose and success should be a roadmap for all. His ability to extrapolate lessons from any situation and thoughtfully apply them to his life is amazing. Great book—it grasped my attention from start to finish."

—Jeff Smith
Leader of The Tactical Empire

"*Don't Run from the Fight* is an excellent book for all men, especially young men looking to build a foundation to withstand life's trials and direct them to greatness. This book lights the way for those who have had to walk into manhood with little guidance. I wish I'd had this book in my earlier years, yet its truths will hold value throughout time."

—Tommy Lam
Cornerstone Building Development

"Eric's *Don't Run from the Fight* is an inspirational, relatable, and empowering tool for any man navigating manhood.

"Having dealt with an absent father myself, while Eric's stories were overwhelmingly analogous, they presented an invitation for greater possibility. Eric is uniquely positioned to speak on this tender and critical subject. He has mastered his own story, found inner strength, and is living his life as a clarion call for other men looking for direction.

"The 'Freedom Framework' is profound enough to touch the most complex of stories yet simple enough for anyone to grasp. Eric provides an actionable, inspiring, truth-centered framework for men to overcome the challenge of their stories and to come out as better men.

"If you are someone struggling with purpose, strength, and victory, *Don't Run from the Fight* is a symphony among the noise in our world."

—Phil Chan, MDiv
Author of *Rhythms of Resilience*

"As a son, husband, father, and friend, this book hit home on many levels. The stories are vivid and enlightening, giving us a fresh perspective on how our past can frame our future for better or worse. The lessons of growth in this book will inspire you and help you inspire those around you."

—Matt Olson
Founder, Move Through Motivation

"Men, if you only read one book this year, let it be *Don't Run from the Fight*. Whether you're struggling with anxiety from the weight of all the responsibility on your shoulders, feeling stuck in your life, or feeling that you're not getting any closer to your goals, Eric's 'Freedom Framework' will help you win the fight.

"Eric has been a longtime friend, a partner in ministry, and even a coach to me. He is also one of the most consistent, generous, and integrity-filled people I know. Believe me when I say that this book was borne out of Eric's true desire to develop men. Eric has helped me to become fit in all aspects of my life—mind, body, and soul—and this book will help get you there too."

—Rev. Roger Lam
Pastor, Missionary, & Social Entrepreneur

"This book is a *game changer*. Eric's story is captivating, and the passion of his words will strike you to the core. The 'Freedom Framework' is about taking ownership of your reactions, questioning them, and adopting a growth mindset towards progress.

"Although the book is directed toward younger men trying to build their story, I believe this book can benefit men of all ages. At forty-one, I have been able to utilize the framework to build a clearer vision of myself and my relationship with my wife and son. I offer my deepest thanks to Eric Freedom for this book."

—Johnny Di Gregorio
Strength and Lifestyle Coach

"I have been following and working with Eric for some time. Not only is he a visionary, but he is also very tactical in this thinking. His knowledge and experience building businesses and helping others have equipped him to meet anyone where they're at while also implementing strategies to get them to the next level toward their goals."

—Shawn Rider
Co-Owner of Shenandoah CrossFit, Mentor, Investor

"Our lives can become consumed with our past hurts. But this book shows us our power to build beyond those memories and become the best and strongest versions of ourselves. What Eric has written here is not only helpful and practical, but it also gives purpose to our pain in a way that breathes new life into each and every day and points us to freedom."

—Mario Quezada
Author, Speaker, Mindset Coach

DON'T RUN
FROM THE
FIGHT

*The Freedom Framework
for Men's Power and Purpose*

ERIC FREEDOM

BERRY
POWELL
PRESS

First paperback edition December 2022
Cover Design by Jazmin Welch and Kay McConnaughey
Interior Design by Formatted Books
Interior Illustrations by Kay McConnaughey
Published by Berry Powell Press
Glendora, California
www.berrypowellpress.com

ISBN: 978-1-7363953-6-3 (paperback)
ISBN: 978-1-7363953-7-0 (ebook)
Library of Congress Control Number: 2021921535

CONTENTS

Strategy Three: Create Your Team

Strategy Four: Challenge Your Story

Strategy Five: Construct Your Future

DEDICATION

To the love of my life, Diana – the one
who turns my doubts into belief, who taught me
that I don't need to be perfect, just present.

To the ones who made me a father – Harper,
Luca, Bailey, may you three brave the world together
to bring it hope and light.

To my father and the fathers who came before
him – each generation has confronted their own
challenges, allowing me to be where I am
at this specific moment in history.

INTRODUCTION

I stepped into the musky, old office full of fold-out chairs. All the faces were unfamiliar, and everyone seemed taller and more confident than me. As a high school freshman, I could tell I was one of the youngest.

Besides being part of athletic teams, this was my first time visiting a group just for teens. My friend Diana (who would eventually become my wife) invited me to go along with her and her friends. At first, I was going to say no. It was so different from anything I'd been to before, and none of *my* friends were going. Then again, I wasn't sure who my friends even were anymore. Honestly, I was pretty lonely, so I said yes, tagging along with Diana and her group.

"All right, now," declared the smiling leader in her bright red shirt. "Grab a chair and make a circle." I hovered nervously near Diana and her friends. We grabbed seats around the circle, but I knew I was out of place.

The leader continued. "As an ice breaker, let's go around the circle and have each of you share your biggest fear."

My mouth fell open. *Are you serious? Tell this group of strangers what I fear most?*

I crossed my arms and looked over at Diana, who seemed relaxed and engaged. *So this is their idea of fun.*

Fortunately for me, we started on the other side of the circle. Others openly shared their fears.

"Spiders!"

"Heights."

"Rollercoasters."

One by one, each person called out their answer with lighthearted ease until it was my turn.

What do I say? I felt all eyes land on me, and my mind was still blank. Diana and the rest of the room stared at me as if to tell me to hurry up. At that exact moment, an answer popped into my mind. Without stopping to think about it, I blurted out, "My biggest fear in life is having no purpose."

The circle went silent. The lanky kid next to me stopped tapping his foot. The leader blinked, not knowing how to handle the situation. After several long moments, the kid on the other side of me said, "Mine is spiders." The circle went on, but the group didn't expect the depth and honesty of my answer. And it certainly took me by surprise as well.

➤ WHY I WROTE THIS BOOK

Growing up is a challenging process. We move through childhood, somehow survive adolescence, and step into adulthood—some with a little more ease than others. My transition has been a bumpy ride, with many obstacles and missteps. The primary questions we must answer are "Who am I?" and "What is my purpose?" These questions are intertwined and are difficult to answer, but this book is about that very thing.

While my answer at the youth group meeting might not have been the most appropriate response for the moment, I don't regret saying it. This strangely personal question asked in this foreign setting prompted a rare moment of clarity and honesty with myself. Not having a purpose *was* my biggest fear. I feared I'd never amount to anything significant. I was a boy with big questions, no answers, and no one to lead me.

Fast-forward to today. I'm in my thirties—a husband, a father of three, a coach, and a fitness entrepreneur of over ten years. I have spent the last decade of my life breaking the cycles of dysfunction I inherited or developed as a response to my pain. My purpose is clear to me, even as it constantly evolves. I have experienced deeper healing in my life and relationships than I ever thought possible. It did not happen in one powerful flash but as a result of taking one step after the other over a long time.

My years of experience as a coach have allowed me to see where my experience connects to larger patterns, particularly those of other young men. When I started my gym, I was trying to help people lose weight, get fit, or train for competition. But the more I worked with my clients, the more I could see that their fitness goals and struggles were deeply intertwined with their identity, worldview, wounds, and fears.

Enmeshed with their fitness journey were their struggles with anger, depression, and bitterness. They wanted to build deeper friendships, felt aimless and anxious about the future, lacked a sense of purpose or security, and constantly sought to feel like they'd done enough. Fitness was the gateway to these deeper issues, and I realized with amazement that I had struggled with all those things too. I felt so alone but knew we were not so different from one another. I thought I could help.

This book is what I needed to read when I was younger. It's for the young man who feels like he needs to be strong but doesn't know how to handle the weak parts of himself. The man who carries a lot on his shoulders and feels like he can't ask for help. The man who feels stuck doing what he's "supposed to do" but longs to find his sense of purpose. As men, we rarely permit ourselves to face these things. As a result, we seldom access the levels of healing and freedom available to us.

The voice of self-doubt constantly questions me. "Who do you think you are to write a book?" But I am a coach at heart—I was born to coach. So I kept coming back to the following idea. Young men need older brother and father figures with whom they can be vulnerable. They need them in their corner, championing them as they strive to become the men they were meant to be.

My purpose in writing this book is to use it to coach younger men as they reach out for a more excellent vision of what they want to do, who they want to be, and how to get there.

➤ FINDING PATTERNS

The foundation of this book builds upon the patterns found in my story and the stories of countless other young men. For one, the fight metaphor is derived from the effort and training required to become the men we want to be. There is an innate resistance to that process that can make growth feel like an uphill battle—but one that's more than worth it.

Second, this large sample of men I've worked with has given me a unique insight into what key factors predict success. They're men of all ages, careers, ethnicities, backgrounds, and stages of life.

I have synthesized those key factors into five major strategies, which I call the "Freedom Framework." This framework is designed to lead you to *real* victory in the *right* fight, without wasting more time on unhelpful strategies or fighting the wrong battles. I did not develop this framework overnight—it took over a decade. It is the culmination of my spiritual, emotional, mental, physical, and financial journey.

While I believe anyone could benefit from this book, I've written it particularly with young men in mind. When I was growing up, I internalized so many destructive messages: I couldn't show weakness, I could only rely on myself, I needed to be a provider above all else, and I needed to fulfill the definition of success that was impressed upon me. I know I'm not the only one. We must unravel these beliefs to ascertain which ones are serving us and which are limiting our freedom.

➤ HOW TO GET THE MOST OUT OF THIS BOOK

Let's talk about how this book is organized. It starts with an introduction to my story and then explains the basic paradigm of the book. This part may read a bit like a memoir, but this is not a memoir. I share my story initially and throughout because I want to be authentic and transparent about what this process entails—at least for me. I hope, in turn, it helps you see your own story with greater lucidity and authenticity.

After this first section, the book is organized by the five major strategies of the Freedom Framework. At the end of each strategy, there is an "Action Plan" to help you implement it in a tangible, approachable way.

For this book to be life-changing, here are a few things I strongly suggest:

1. Read the strategies in order, then skip around as needed.

The five strategies don't exist in a strict step-by-step order because growth does not happen in a linear progression, let alone the same for each person. That said, the concepts and stories presented here build on one another. It's helpful to read it in order, then go back to whatever you need to hear or be reminded of as needed.

2. Go slowly and honestly.

You have permission to bring your full self—all your questions, thoughts, uncertainties, and fears. In fact, you *need* to bring your full self to get the full benefits of this book. Take advantage of this space where there is nothing to hide. Take a deep breath and take your time. Be as honest as you can.

3. Complete the Action Plans at the end of each strategy.

These questions and prompts are designed for your victory. They exist to help you move from the conceptual to the practical, so the substance of this book can move from your mind into your life, habits, and relationships. They are simply a starting point, but taking that starting point is invaluable.

4. Don't do this alone.

A fighter does not train, let alone enter the ring alone. A solitary growth journey is inherently stunted. Inviting someone else into our growth can be difficult, but as you begin this book, ask someone to read it with you. Gather a group. At the very least, find one other person you feel safe with and share with them what you're learning.

❯ A FINAL NOTE

Many authors have told me that it never feels like a book is finished. It can always be improved, and it's hard to let go of the desire to add or change what's on the page. But now comes the time when I let go of this manuscript that only a few select people have read and allow it to become a book that is available to the public. It's a bold move, one that honestly scares me.

One of the many challenges of writing this book was describing how growth happens. Growth is convoluted, multi-dimensional, and intuitive, while a book is linear with a beginning, a middle, and an end. It's a difficult task, and I hope I did it well enough to help make a difference in my readers' lives.

Another difficulty is that I am indebted to many people who helped me on this journey. I wrote this book over the course of two years, and most of its themes come from my last two decades of growth. My name is on the cover, and it feels like an overstatement. It's not as if the learning within the pages came from me alone. I will never be able to fully credit every source of transformation that shaped me in the last two decades. Much of the wisdom was gleaned from other powerful leaders, writers, and coaches, and it's impossible to capture all their wisdom here. It's important to mention that my faith and relationship with God has transformed a great deal of my story—it defies the capacity of my language, let alone a single book.

That said, through all the years and conversations and bathroom-floor prayers, what remained consistent was taking the next step. So despite the limitations of this book and myself, I pray this book will help you to do just that—take the next step, whatever that is for you.

Besides the vulnerability of writing a book, all the stories I share are very personal. I made difficult decisions on which stories to use as illustrations and which to leave out. The most powerful stories are from my own life, which were difficult to share, as I want to protect those closest to me. To that end, all the stories in this book are based on real people, but I've changed some names and details to protect people's privacy when applicable. However, I knew this book would not challenge you to reach into the deepest places of your heart if I didn't share from the depth of my own.

I can't wait to journey with you through this book. Throughout these pages, I will entrust you with parts of my life I've only shared with my closest friends. As you read, I believe your story will become more and more clear. Maybe ours will be very similar; maybe they couldn't be more different. Regardless, I believe you will notice your own story knocking at the door of your heart. When it does, I encourage you to answer it with honesty. Let's do this.

Eric Freedom

HOW I DEVELOPED THE FREEDOM FRAMEWORK

1

THE DAY MY WORLD FLIPPED ON ITS HEAD

Life begins on the other side of despair.
—JEAN-PAUL SARTRE

BANG!

An explosion went off outside.

"What was that?" My five-year-old brother Patrick turned to me with wide brown eyes, jabbing his scrawny elbows into the couch.

"I'm not sure," I responded. I was only ten, but my gut told me something was wrong.

"Where's mom?" his voice came out squeaky, like the cartoon voices still playing on the TV.

I jumped up from the pale blue couch. "I think she's outside working in the yard."

Why did it sound so close?

"Stay on the couch," I told my brother. He sat obediently.

I quickly crossed the living room, wove through the kitchen, and opened the screen door toward the garage outside. Before I could turn the corner, I heard a second bang.

That's when I knew for certain I'd just heard two gunshots. I slowly pushed past the door toward the wooden fence where I could see for myself. Shaking, I took my next few steps, not knowing what type of horror I might find around the corner.

My mom was crouched against the bumper of our family station wagon, shaking and crying. Opposite her on the manicured lawn stood my father, who I'd not seen for days. His face was so distorted with rage that he looked like a stranger to me. Who could I call for help? The protector of my family now stood holding a gun in his shaky hand, screaming obscenities at my mom as she wept. But there was no blood. He had fired twice and missed twice.

I turned around and bolted back inside. I knew I wasn't supposed to see what I just saw. Patrick was still watching TV. I sat beside him, and we both stared blankly, saying nothing.

Minutes later, our mom burst through the kitchen door. She ran past us in the living room and down the hall into my parents' bedroom. I heard the door slam shut, lock, and heavy objects clunking on the other side. She was barricading herself in.

My father burst through the door next, not even looking at us. We sat, like good children, as he pounded his fists against the splintering wood. He was screaming, trying to explain himself. My mom must have called my dad's brother and father because they arrived within minutes. My dad got through the door somehow, but moments later, my uncle and grandfather barreled in, and the two pinned him down in the narrow hallway. I don't remember how they got him to leave, but eventually, they drove him away. No authorities were called, and no arrests were made. The house was quiet again.

➤ MY PARENTS' STORY DEFINED MY STORY

Before this day, I thought I knew my place in the world. I was the eldest of two sons, born to proud, hardworking, first-generation Taiwanese immigrants. My parents met in the U.S. when my dad walked through the door of my mom's garment shop, trying to sell her a fax machine. Both were in their twenties and looking to establish their lives here. There was a quick courtship before they married and started a family consisting of my younger brother and me. They built a successful real estate business together, chasing the American Dream.

As a boy, I looked up to my dad. Despite the narrow options available to Asian immigrants in the late seventies to early eighties, he was the epitome of a winner. While there was still a great deal of distrust toward immigrants, the cultural explosion of Bruce Lee and Jackie Chan movies worked in his favor. Since my dad had his eighth-degree black belt, the primarily Caucasian students at Seattle University easily associated him with these martial arts stars. Using the stereotype to his advantage, my father launched his first successful business teaching martial arts classes for other students. They were lucrative, as was his side-hustle selling uniforms, belts, and other martial arts equipment he imported from overseas. My dad might not have been the highest achiever academically, but he was *always* entrepreneurial. Where there were no open doors, my dad created opportunities for himself. From his life, I learned a strong work ethic, to think outside the box, and to use my creativity.

My mother was just as industrious. When I was little, she told me stories about how her father grew up in a cave. I didn't believe her. A dirt floor, with rock over his head? There was no way—until I finally saw pictures of it. It really was a cave. With the little her parents could provide for her, my mother worked several jobs and saved up the money to come to America. Once she arrived, my mother started working at a garment store, building her life from the ground up. When she and my father started their business out of the garage, she handled all the accounting. While my father may have overshadowed her personality and role, she had every bit as much grit and skill.

> Where there were no open doors, my dad created opportunities for himself. From his life, I learned a strong work ethic, to think outside the box, and to use my creativity.

By the time I was in the fifth grade, I'd adopted the creative work ethic I'd seen modeled by my parents. That year, I burst onto the entrepreneurial scene by starting a few businesses. First, I sold Airheads taffy candies. Back when Costco was still called Price Club, I would persuade my mom to take me there on a Saturday and buy a box. I would disperse the box of Airheads into three one-gallon zip lock bags. Two friends and I would sling Airheads during recess and after school—seventy-five cents apiece or two for a dollar. My little enterprise was killing it, raking in fifty dollars a week after I paid commissions to my friends. I was hustling!

It didn't stop there. I funneled this cash into my next money-makers—baseball cards and POGs (collectible cardboard bottlecaps). They were both huge in the early nineties. I bought boxes of each and sold them to my friends.

If you're a basketball fan, you may especially appreciate this next endeavor—my biggest hustle yet. In sixth grade, I scored a Vince Carter Rookie FX card for seven dollars. I sent the card in to be graded, and then I sold it back to a local trading card store for *six hundred dollars*. They paid me in one-dollar bills. I never ran home so fast in my life. The next morning, I bought all my friends as many bags of chips as they wanted at the liquor store down the street from our school. I felt like a hero.

Before my dad moved out, I found a stash of magazines under my dad's side of the bed. That allowed me to expand my inventory even further. I had Penthouse, Hustler—you name it. It was the equivalent of twenty-four karat gold for a preadolescent teen. I was still in middle school when I took those magazines and leased them out for rent during recess breaks—two dollars per minute. I made more money than most ten-year-old kids might dream of having.

All of this was to follow in my parents' footsteps. I saw their hard work—long hours and weekends, even holidays. Seeing their entrepreneurial history, I desired to start a business, run side hustles, and make money to buy what I wanted. My parents defined my reality, and I internalized their expectations for me. I adopted their values and goals as my own.

> My parents defined my reality, and I internalized their expectations for me. I adopted their values and goals as my own.

—

While I kept busy hustling at school, my parents' marriage unraveled behind closed doors. Neither of my parents had the emotional or relational tools to resolve the trauma they had individually experienced throughout their lifetimes. My brother and I turned up the television a little louder, pretending we didn't know what they didn't want to acknowledge. Yet the shouting matches were hardly muffled by the thin walls of our home. The icy looks they exchanged were not lost on us. Their distance grew.

Suddenly, my dad moved out at the height of my ten-year-old business career. The pretense of domestic peace shattered the day of the gunshots—the explosive moment where everything hidden was laid out for everyone to see. Our friends and family saw it all—the rage, regret, pain, despair, and violence without any way of reconciliation.

While our mother hid in her room, our Auntie ushered us to the round kitchen table. "Here, eat." She placed two bowls in front of us—a Chinese noodle dish with mustard greens and sliced pork. It was pungent and soupy, one of my favorites. It smelt like home, even though nothing felt like home anymore. My brother and I just looked at the bowls, and then my brother turned to me. He said nothing. His eyes did the asking. "What's happening?" I returned his silent gaze. I had no answer for him. I sat there equally confused, stunned, and helpless.

I couldn't sleep that night, so I got up and creaked open my mom's bedroom door. She was awake and motioned for me to sit next to her on her bed. She was wrapped in a robe, her eyes puffy and red behind her glasses. She looked like she had gone to war.

She leaned in toward my face, looking at me seriously, and asked, "You remember the movie *Man of the House*? The one with Chevy Chase?"

I was caught off guard. It was a recent Disney comedy where an eleven-year-old boy builds a new life with his mom after his father leaves. The boy employed some funny hijinks to keep her from remarrying.

I blinked at her. "Yeah, I remember it."

"Well, that's you now. You're the new man of the house, okay?"

She explained, "Your dad will not be around much anymore. I need you to be a man for your brother, and I need you to listen to what I say more than ever. And I need to know you're not going to get into trouble at school and run in the wrong circles."

I nodded quietly, asking no questions.

➤ WHO AM I NOW?

In one afternoon, the person I thought I was had been redefined for me. Sure, I was still the eldest of two sons, born to proud, hardworking, first-generation Taiwanese immigrants. But now, I would be raised by a single mother because my father had tried to hurt her. In the days to come, my parents would get what is crudely referred to as an "Asian divorce," meaning they were together on paper and financially, but they lived separately. I was now the man of the house and responsible for my little brother. At ten years old, I felt this weight settle onto my shoulders. My dad was gone, and I was the one who needed to fill his empty shoes. How was I supposed to know how to do that?

No one took the time to explain what was going on to my brother and me. Without explanation, Patrick and I made up answers that made sense to us. We wanted to ask, of course, but there was a touchy, off-limits feeling around the topic. We didn't ask questions. Before the day of the gunshots, we weren't blind to the tension rising between our parents, but we assumed they'd work it out. Our mom had told us everything was fine, so we assumed it was. That made it even more jarring when it was suddenly and obviously anything but fine. After all, I could have lost my mom that day, and anything that could have led to that was not fine at all. That planted a deep fear in me that life as I knew it was not stable—it could irreversibly change on a dime with no warning.

This event also caused me to question everything I thought was safe. My dad was supposed to be my protector—*our* protector. But when the hero of the movie becomes a villain, who comes in to save you? Who flies in to pick up the pieces? He and my mom were supposed to be a team, the two of them like a shelter over our heads. Now, that shelter collapsed on top of us, leaving us dazed and bruised, our family shattered in the aftermath. I didn't know what it meant to be safe anymore. I decided that I'd have to rely on myself to be safe. I couldn't trust anyone anymore.

Not only did I lose my protector, but I also lost my hero. My father was my role model for what it meant to be a man. I now had no idea what it meant to be a man, although I had already learned so much from him. How was I to know what parts to keep and what parts to throw out? I tried to reject him entirely, but his values, habits, and worldview still tinted my reality like a pair of glasses I didn't know I was wearing.

While I had previously felt anchored in who I was, who I thought my family was, and the kind of person I wanted to be, I now felt anchorless. I didn't know who

I was, where to find safety, who I could trust, or who I wanted to be. My dad was gone, and I struggled to fill his empty shoes. I had to grow up fast but without a role model or mentor. My friends were ten, so they had no idea how to help me suddenly turn into a man. I became my mother's counterpart in the household, and I felt completely on my own.

2

THE FIVE KEY STRATEGIES
OF GROWTH

*Anger is an assertion of rights and worth. In anger,
whether you like it or not, there is truth.*

—SOROYA CHEMALY

Only some have such a jarring introduction to growing up. Most boys have time to get through middle school and take a few years in high school to figure things out. You may have had a smoother transition than I have. But then you may also have stories of abrupt transition and trauma that have complicated your shift to adulthood.

My journey has been challenging and unpredictable. I'm now in my thirties, and it's hard to believe it's been well over twenty years since that fateful day when I abruptly became a ten-year-old "man of the house." I was on the fast track with no guard rails.

When my parents eventually got divorced, the assets were divided. My dad got the real estate business my parents had built together; my mom got the two of us and the house. The fighting was over with my mom, my brother, and me at home. The halls were quieter. It felt peaceful, in a way—better than pretending to be a traditional family when we weren't. Gone were the awkward car rides where my parents argued over money as my brother and I sat silently in the back seat.

On the other hand, the quiet reminded us of what we'd lost. I missed my dad, or rather, I missed having a dad I could look up to and follow. But over time, my childlike confusion and grief hardened into rage and resentment, which focused solely on my father. Even though my dad lived twenty minutes away, he was non-existent in my life. That was my choice. I'd refused to see him. He had no "joint custody" over me, as far as I was concerned. He'd take my little brother from time to time while I stayed home. I envisioned the day when I would grow big and strong enough to put him in his place. That day came one afternoon when I was a sophomore in high school.

➤ LIVING WITH CLENCHED FISTS

I sat at the kitchen table. I spread my elbows across the smooth wood, homework papers splayed out before me. It was quiet except for the scribbling of my pencil—until I heard a knock at the door.

That's odd. I slid out from my chair. No one else was supposed to be home until later. I wasn't even supposed to be home, except my after-school plan had fallen through. *Maybe it's the mailman.*

I opened the door and saw my father standing on the steps in front of me. He was not the person I was expecting to see, and he looked surprised too.

"What are you doing here?" I asked harshly.

"Just dropping off your brother," my dad said.

I studied my father's face, staring at new stubble on his chin.

Patrick was supposed to be with my father for the rest of the day. My brother's shoulders slouched; he wore the same look he always did when he returned from our dad's—disappointment. A fire was already smoldering inside me. No one spoke for a moment.

"You're not supposed to be here for another four hours. Why are you here now?"

Dad didn't respond. Anticipating tension, my little brother wriggled between me and the doorframe, shrugged off his backpack, and darted to his room.

"I wasn't even supposed to be home right now. Mom won't be home until tonight. That's why you were supposed to have him!"

Again, he said nothing.

He would have dropped off my brother early, even if there was no one home. As my brain processed that irresponsibility, the smoldering inside me burst into flames.

"He would have been home alone for *hours*. He's *ten*! What if I wasn't home? What if something happened to him?" I raised my voice at him, raging on my brother's behalf.

Then I felt a coldness flow over me. My face hardened into a stone-cold glare, clenching my fists at my sides. He took notice. He stepped toward me and stuck his face an inch away from mine. I could feel the breath coming out of his nose. Dad smelt like cologne and cigarettes, as he always did.

"What's your problem? What, you gonna hit me?"

Years ago, this would have silenced me. But now, I was almost as tall as him and in good shape from playing travel basketball. I put my shoulders back, blocking the entryway to my house.

Staying an inch from his face, I said, "Get out of my house. You don't live here anymore."

His face twisted with anger, but there was a flash of surprise in his eyes. He held still for a moment, unsure of what to do next. It felt good to catch him off guard.

Finally, he scoffed and turned away. Apparently, it was not worth the fight.

I watched him walk back down the driveway and get into his car. I stood in the doorway, arms crossed, with my brother behind me. My father was the one who backed down this time. I felt like I'd won.

▸ FIGHTING THE WRONG BATTLES

I sat back down at the table and expected to feel strong and triumphant. I'd dreamt of this day—when I would be big and strong enough to put my dad in his place and show him he didn't scare me anymore. I'd been waiting for the day I could stand up to him.

This victorious feeling lasted for about sixty seconds. Despite feeling like I'd won by being stronger and more aggressive than my dad, I only felt worse. I hadn't expected to react this way. I didn't feel any better about myself. I was just as angry, if not angrier. Afterward, I was plagued by wondering what he thought of me now. I couldn't shake the ache of longing for his approval, no matter how much I resented him. Another sickening thought settled in my stomach—was I becoming just as bad as him? I convinced myself I was only protecting my family, but I still felt queasy. This wasn't how a winner was supposed to feel, was it? No, it was not. So why did I feel so horrible? I didn't understand it.

I continued to struggle without knowing why. Grasping for answers, I found more and more "opponents" to blame. My father was first, and I blamed him for any obstacle or shortcoming for which I didn't have another explanation. I blamed my coaches when I didn't make the varsity basketball team freshman year. I blamed my lack of natural intellect when I got rejected from the schools I applied to. I blamed my heritage and financial status when I struggled to take risks. When my marriage was in turmoil, I blamed my family history of divorce. My cadre of opponents grew.

I battled these opponents ferociously, screaming at my dad, blowing up at my coaches, overworking to save more money, and studying hard to get into a good school. I wanted to win and make them lose, thinking I'd feel better about myself. Yet no victory in any of these areas could fill my underlying emptiness.

Looking back, I realize I was dissatisfied because I instinctively knew something was off. It would be years before I had the insight to know what that something was—I was fighting the wrong battles. Lacking complete understanding, I continued wasting my energy and time. I was battling for surface-level victories without ever addressing the root of my struggle. On top of that, I was alienating many people in my life. I became known as a guy with an awful temper. I didn't get the respect I thought winning would achieve.

> The real fight I needed to face was not overpowering my father or anyone else; my real war was inside of me. I needed to take control over what I believed about myself and who I could become.

The real fight I needed to face was not overpowering my father or anyone else; my real war was inside of me. I needed to take control over what I believed about myself and who I could become. I needed to win the battle of healing from pain and to win my freedom from the past. I thought of myself as a fighter, but when facing the heart of my real fight, I ran the other way. It took years for me to face the fight that would determine my future.

➤ FREEDOM TO CHOOSE MY TRAJECTORY

Fast forward to 2019, when I attended a men's retreat focused on personal and spiritual growth. Eighty men piled into cars, from young adults to guys in their sixties. Many were young dads like me, also reveling in the fact that they managed to pull this weekend off.

Within the span of two hours, we broke free from the city traffic and concrete landscape of the freeway, pulling onto a route that would take us up into the mountains that border the outer Los Angeles perimeter. Before long, we were cruising up windy roads, the concrete landscape giving way to the granite mountainside, scrappy native plants, and dazzling views of the city in the distance. We arrived just as the sun was setting.

We spread out in the main room, spacious and cabin-like with log walls and round tables. We took our seats, and I exhaled deeply, feeling the week's worries beginning to unravel.

Throughout those two days, we listened to speakers and did group activities, but what I remember most is a moment on the last night. One of the retreat leaders asked us to choose a word to represent what would be leaving the mountain with us.

Suddenly and clearly, the word "freedom" displayed in my mind. It immediately felt right. I scribbled it into my leather journal. I looked at its presence, floating between the blue lines, and tried to understand why it resonated so profoundly. Tears brimmed in my eyes.

When I saw this word, "Freedom," I felt like I was writing myself a permission slip. I'd defined myself all my life by loss, pain, and others' expectations. I was trapped for so long, and I had created a story about myself that set me up to be the loser. Sure, I was physically strong. But what had that gotten me?

The burden I'd been carrying was the impossible goal of living up to (or maybe down to) other people's expectations. I'd accepted the story that I'd been told: I wasn't smart enough, I wasn't rich enough, and I simply wasn't enough of whatever it took to live a life with purpose and healthy relationships.

But as I read that word again, "Freedom," I realized it was the word that now defined me. I was no longer identified by fear, loss, and pain. I didn't have to stumble under a burden I was never meant to carry. I was not an angry person anymore who didn't know how to manage his feelings. I didn't alienate people, but instead, I nurtured other people. It was a moment of release and gratitude. I was free.

➤ THE FREEDOM FRAMEWORK FOR WINNING YOUR FIGHT

Do you know what freedom feels like? To be free of what other people think of you? To have opportunities you didn't think could open for you? To be able to define yourself on your terms, no longer tying your self-worth to your status, accomplishments, or others' expectations? To feel genuine peace with the past and clarity and purpose toward the future? That is the freedom we will work toward through these pages.

I want to share how I learned to fight the right fight, *the good fight*, and to win at being exactly the man I was meant to be. Today, I'm the founder of a constantly growing gym and community called Reason Fitness. I was married in 2012 to my wife, Diana, and we have three small children. Like everyone else, our lives with three children five and under often feel chaotic. But I feel a piercing sense of contentment and incisiveness about who I am and why I am here. I am confident that I can tailor my decisions to align with reality and achieve my goals. I'm able to be the person—coach, husband, father, and friend—that I'm designed to be.

> I want to share how I learned to fight the right fight, *the good fight*, and to win at being exactly the man I was meant to be.

As I mentioned in the introduction, my years as a fitness coach have shown me that many young men experience similar struggles to the ones I've faced. The more I worked with my fitness clients, the more I saw that their concerns were more profound than the physical ones—they had questions about their value and purpose. Many felt entangled by family wounds that strangled their current relationships. Many felt trapped by the expectations of others or even their expectations of themselves. Many had a sense of their purpose but felt unstable and uncertain of how to actualize it. Many felt stable and successful but wondered if that was all there was. Most of all, many felt stuck in a rut, wrestling with anger, depression, bitterness, and anxiousness. They longed for growth but knew they were stuck in specific patterns that no longer served them.

As I continued to work with clients and explore my personal history, I began to understand more about this struggle and what strategies proved effective in sustaining actual growth. Of those strategies, I chose the five that revealed themselves as essential. I've organized this book by them, which I call the Freedom Framework.

The goal of the Freedom Framework is to help you identify your fight, develop the inner tools to face it, gather the support you need, begin to redefine your story, and take steps toward a new future. I've designed these strategies to prompt self-discovery and provide tangible tools to implement transformation in your mind, habits, and relationships.

The following are the main objectives for each of the five strategies.

Strategy One: Commit to Win

> Increase awareness of your own story
> Identify what your fight is in this season of life
> Develop a vivid vision for what winning would look like

Strategy Two: Claim Your Power

> ➤ Debunk myths of emotion and masculinity
> ➤ Regain power over your inner world
> ➤ Gain tools to regulate emotions

Strategy Three: Create Your Team

> ➤ Identify barriers to connection
> ➤ Understand why other men are critical to your victory
> ➤ Create an inner circle to help you win

Strategy Four: Challenge Your Story

> ➤ Establish a core sense of identity that withstands external change
> ➤ Recognize dissonance between your values and actions
> ➤ Create new patterns to back your new identity

Strategy Five: Construct Your Future

> ➤ Clarify your purpose amid countless options
> ➤ Develop a mindset for continuous growth
> ➤ Take tangible steps toward a new reality

While I believe anyone could benefit from this framework, I've written this book particularly with young men in mind. (Love ya ladies, but this one's for the boyssss.) In short, I've written intending to create the book I needed when I was younger. I see a desperate need for more men who can lead others to face the heaviest issues of their hearts and minds. We need more men who permit us to go there, stand beside us in the valleys, and model what to do when we get to those places. Only then can we access the levels of healing and freedom available to us. We become the brothers, husbands, fathers, followers, friends, and leaders we were made to be.

While this book applies to any age group, I've also written it with young adults in mind. That season of life was when I first discovered my fight, and there is a good reason for that. Squarely out of childhood and just entering adulthood, this juncture is where we decide what our past will mean for our future. At this stage, we have the distance necessary to give us a new perspective on our formative years. Not only that, but our brains are fully or almost entirely developed at the average age of twenty-five. That means our brains have a greater capacity for critical thinking, empathy, insight, and reflection than they have ever physically been capable of before. We are old enough to where we can now act on this new understanding, usually without being under the control of our parents. However, we're young enough to be malleable. It's much easier to break a habit or mindset after five years than after fifty. This combination of factors makes young adulthood a ripe age to question the stories we've been given and decide who we'd like to be in the world. I will walk you through my journey through these years in the hope it will prompt insight, clarity, and direction toward your own.

This book is for the man who:

> Feels like he needs to be strong but doesn't know how to handle the parts of himself that feel weak

> Feels stuck trying to do what he's "supposed to do" but longs to find his sense of purpose

> Is hungry to go deeper in the inner workings of his emotions and relationships but doesn't have the language or tools to do so

> Wants to adopt mindsets and create habits that will carry him toward his life goals in the upcoming decade(s) but lacks a role model or a place to start

The Freedom Framework is rigorous and demanding. You'll confront things you may be currently trying to avoid. And like any fight, you'll need to understand your opponent, train for the competition, and be completely committed to winning. Parts of the process will feel uncomfortable and maybe even bring up pain points. But I hope you find it exhilarating to understand more about yourself, connect to what matters, and uncover who you are destined to be in this world.

It has taken me a long time to be willing to take responsibility for my life or openly acknowledge what I've been through, including my mistakes and successes I've achieved. But I'm going to share my story with you in the hopes that you'll see yourself in it somewhere and be able to use some of the same strategies I've used to stop running from the fight and face life head-on.

You can continue living without questioning the stories, values, and concerns your family, community, and society gave you. These can be quite limiting, disempowering, or ill-fitting at best. Or you can intentionally expand your options and define the man you want to become.

ACTION PLAN:
OWN YOUR STORY

In the following chapter, we will explore the nature of the fight more in-depth. But first, I want you to take stock of your own story. It will help you identify themes and patterns and see where greater freedom is available to you in subsequent chapters. I hope reading my story here brings yours forth more clearly. If it's helpful, use mine as a starting point. I encourage you to take a few minutes, grab a pen, and answer the questions below.

1. What do our stories have in common if anything?
2. How is your story different from mine?
3. Were there events in your childhood that forced you to grow up quicker?
4. What were some common topics of conversation within your family of origin?
5. Which discussion topics were off-limits within your family of origin?
6. What values did your family of origin pass on to you?

STRATEGY ONE:

COMMIT TO WIN

COMMIT TO WIN

3

THE SINGLE GREATEST PREDICTOR OF SUCCESS

Change happens when the pain of staying the same is greater than the pain of change.

—TONY ROBBINS

As soon as I heard my wife Diana's footsteps, I met her at the door with my shoes on, coat in hand. Eagerly I asked, "You ready for the movie?" We'd planned to see *Zero Dark 30* for date night (my choice), and I'd been looking forward to it all week.

The door opened slowly. Eyes weary, shoulders slouched, bag overflowing with papers—Diana wore all the signs of exhaustion. She was a fifth-grade teacher returning from her hour-and-a-half commute. Panic shot through me, anticipating her answer.

"I'm so tired." She pushed frazzled hairs away from her face and dropped her overstuffed leather bag on the bench seat by the door. "I just want to order some pizza and go to bed."

I blinked and responded slowly, still posted by the door. "So you *don't* want to go to the movie?"

"Yeah, I mean, if you don't mind. I want to relax."

I stared blankly as she took off her shoes, moved past me, and collapsed deep into the embrace of our leather couch.

My body started to feel numb. "I really—I really wanted to watch the movie." Still frozen in our doorway, I burst into tears. I was bawling—not just sniffling—full-on sobbing.

"Wait, are you crying?" she sat up, her face peeking over the couch back. I turned toward the wall; my face felt hot as unwelcome tears blurred my vision.

"This must be the best movie of all time," she said with confusion. She couldn't hide her surprise. My anger was familiar, but my tears were an anomaly. She stood up and met me back in the doorway, putting her hand on my back.

The words that came out of my mouth next surprised me. I didn't speak them so much as they tumbled out on their own. "I hate my life. I hate my life."

Diana looked even more confused, even a little hurt. I tried to clarify as more words poured out of me.

"You know I love you. I don't regret our marriage. That's not what I mean. In truth, that's the only thing I feel happy about. That and coaching at night. Outside of those four hours, I feel so miserable. It's just same shit, different day. I literally wake up every day and hate my life."

My sobs grew heavier until I gasped for air. I calmed myself and I sat on the bench, lifeless as the coats hanging on the rack beside me. "I thought my life would look one way, and here I am on the opposite side of the spectrum from where I thought I'd be. I figured everything would be okay if I just took this job from my dad. We could pay off debt, save up, and maybe things would get better with him!" Another sob broke out. "But I hate working there. I hate real estate. I'm just miserable."

Her face softened. She stayed beside me with her hand on my back, looking at me as I fixated on a particular floorboard.

"I want to escape. I don't want to think about my life. I want to go to this movie and watch the Navy Seals for two hours because it's better than thinking about all this bullshit. It's better than the reality I'm living in right now."

She stayed silent for a minute and then, with both hands, lifted my face to look at her. Her eyes surprised me—they were not sad or sympathetic; they were clear and resolute.

"I think you should open your gym."

"What?" I wiped my face with both hands.

"I think we should forget our five-year plan. You should open your gym now."

"Now? What about all our student debt and my dad? I can't start a gym right now. I can't do that right now."

She didn't seem to hear me. "I think this is the time. I think you should go all in on this. I believe this would make you happy. Plus, Eric, you're an excellent coach."

She looked into my eyes and soul and spoke sweetly. "I think you should do it."

› THE DAY I STOPPED RUNNING

How did I end up a full-grown man weeping because I couldn't go to the movies? Behind that moment were years of running, ignoring, avoiding, and distracting. I broke down when I did because I never allowed myself to do so sooner. Now, I had no choice, and the fight I'd been avoiding had finally caught up with me.

Let me give you some backstory. A few years before, I graduated from college with a degree in kinesiology, and I had no idea where to go next. I had fallen in love with CrossFit, was coaching guys out of my garage, and fantasized about owning a gym one day. At heart, I was a coach, but I didn't think there was any way I could make a living coaching full-time. I felt aimless. The blank slate before me was terrifying.

Then, my dad called me out of the blue. We hadn't talked in forever. Our relationship was one of push and shove, which is why his following words caught me so off guard.

"I know it's hard getting a job after college," he said. "I'd like you to come to work for me." It was a position at the real estate business he and my mom created. I could not have cared less about real estate, and I still didn't trust him. But the pay was stable, Diana and I were trying to pay off our debt, and it seemed like an "adult job." I reasoned I could swallow my pride and make "the responsible choice." I took the job.

Three years later, however, I was miserable. Some days it felt like I was hanging on by a thread. I didn't admit that, of course. I wore a guise that I was balancing it all successfully. But beneath the surface, I was slowly dying.

First, I hated working in real estate. I wasn't bad at it—I was on track to keep moving up in the company. But I had no passion for it, and my desk felt like jail. I worked two side jobs in fitness, creating a sixty-hour work week. But while they weren't "real jobs," as my dad said, my side jobs were the only work that made me feel alive. I spent every hour of my real job wishing I was somewhere else.

I had another hidden motivation that was making the job even more unbearable. Despite my resentment towards my dad, I still wanted him to be proud of me. Work had always been the sole object of my dad's attention. Deep down, I thought if I became part of his work world, I could also win some of that attention. But succeeding in his industry didn't mend our relationship like I had hoped. Working together stirred even more tension, churning up old wounds and aggravating them rather than healing them.

On the surface, it seemed like I was doing everything right. Wasn't I? I was newly married, working more than full time right out of college, moving my way up in a real estate company, and paying off debt. And I was helping with the family business like a good son. Like the confrontation with my dad at the door years before, I thought, "This isn't what winning is supposed to feel like!" These "victories" left me feeling empty.

Rather than stopping to face this emptiness—study it, understand it, and begin to heal—I just kept building a façade on top of it. I kept myself busy, overworking, racking up external success, and playing the role others expected me to. I stuffed down my discontentment until it eventually exploded in anger or tears, hurting myself or those around me. Without realizing it, my avoidance pattern led me down the exact same path that led to my father's greatest mistake.

This breakdown was the day I stopped running. It wasn't a choice; it was because I simply couldn't run anymore. I could no longer pretend I was okay. The pain that raged inside me was too big to keep avoiding. All my crutches—entertainment, achievement, overworking—collapsed. My numbing agents had worn off. My mask of having it together as a man was ripped off. Trying to be a provider, I was burning out. Trying to chase security, I felt empty. Trying to appear strong, I felt isolated. Trying to stifle my emotions, I pushed my pain deeper. I could no longer deny it: I would run myself into the ground if I didn't act now. It was finally time to face my real fight.

❯ DISCOVERING THE REAL FIGHT

What is the real fight? What did I need to face to claim the authentic victory I had longed for since childhood? Throwing punches, compiling achievements, or meeting expectations could not win my real fight.

My real fight was with myself. *I* was the one who needed to change.

What was keeping me from the change that would set me free? From what exactly was I running?

I wasn't running from freedom; I was running from the discomfort it would take to achieve that freedom. All the time I spent avoiding my fight, avoiding the root of the problem, I was running from discomfort.

That may sound strange. After all, I wasn't in a comfortable position to begin with—or was I? I wanted to dominate my dad and others in physical strength because I felt most comfortable being the most powerful person in the room. Taking the job at my dad's company was far more comfortable than risking it in uncharted territory.

> Throwing punches, compiling achievements, or meeting expectations could not win my real fight. My real fight was with myself. *I* was the one who needed to change.

Living up to my parents' expectations was more comfortable than breaking the mold. Seeking my dad's approval was more comfortable than accepting I might never have it. I was more comfortable overworking than learning how to rest. Taking everything onto my shoulders was more comfortable than asking for help. Rather than sitting down and being vulnerable about what I felt and why, I was more comfortable exploding in rage. And isolating myself was more comfortable than inviting someone else into my mess. Every major decision I made was in service of this avoidance.

By making these decisions, I set myself up for a level of pain that I eventually could not endure—not physically or emotionally. When we try to avoid the discomfort of growth, we always end up causing more suffering and injury to ourselves and others, making a bigger mess out of our lives.

› WHAT IS THE FIGHT?

The fight is the act of overcoming the discomfort of growth.

It is the battle against the force of normalcy, complacency, and the status quo. It is an active resistance to passively repeating the story we were given without questioning it long enough to begin writing our own. When we face our fight, we press into that discomfort to claim our freedom on the other side. It's not a physical battle with winners and losers—it's an internal battle where we're only up against ourselves.

> The greatest predictor of success is the capacity to handle discomfort.

To understand fully what the fight is, we must understand the following statement. This may be the most important statement I make in this book: The greatest predictor of success is the capacity to handle discomfort.

GREATER SUCCESS = GREATER CAPACITY FOR DISCOMFORT

COMFORT ZONE

GROWTH ZONE

ROAD TO SUCCESS

REQUIRES STAMINA

What does this look like, practically speaking? To identify our fight is to identify the root issue we don't want to face in a particular situation or season. It's not a singular event or isolated to one area of our lives. Rather, it's an ongoing process of identifying what's holding us back and training ourselves to overcome that discomfort. We can ask ourselves what we need to press into to grow our marriages, careers, family lives, emotional health, and physical fitness. While each season of life may come with a different emphasis, the fight paradigm gives us a way of seeing the root issue and taking ownership of it. That is what I designed the Freedom Framework to help us attain—the growth and freedom available to us when we win the fight against discomfort.

How is it that discomfort can be the root of our fight? Let me give an illustration through the lens of our physical bodies. Say you feel pain in your knee, and now it hurts when you walk. You don't want to deal with having to go to the doctor and having it looked at immediately. So, what happens? You decide to tolerate it. You avoid dealing with it.

The body is an amazing instrument and a metaphor for life. When one part of the body is injured, it throws the rest off balance. You adjust how you walk to avoid putting pressure on the knee because it hurts. Now, one side of your body carries more weight than the other. Your other knee starts hurting, and you feel pain in your upper back. You take Advil or use Icy Hot to try and soothe it, but it keeps coming back. You've created a situation now that is causing harm to other parts of your body and is much more painful than the original injury.

How do we fix the problem? First, we need to go to the source, back to the knee injury that started this domino effect of pain. Anyone who has experienced physical therapy will tell you that when you go back to mend that initial injury, it is *not* comfortable. Healing that knee will require prolonged time and attention, moving it in ways it does not want to be moved. The muscles experience stress, tearing, and soreness, just as when working out.

However, the discomfort we lean into trains or retrains the body to move the way it's supposed to again. If we can't tolerate the misery of the healing process, we will forever limp.

Everything we want is on the other side of discomfort. Every time we desire growth, we will need to go through some uncomfortable things to get it. Think about it. We want energy—strong, healthy bodies to lift our kids high above our heads. We want thriving relationships—marriages that nourish us and friendships that last. We want to fulfill our individual sense of purpose—start that business, write that book, and follow that idea to see where it goes. We want whole families—to love and be loved freely by those who gave us life. Writing this book has been one of the most uncomfortable experiences of all! But for every single one of our dreams to become a reality, we need to put in the work. We need to work against the status quo of our internal selves and our external worlds. Nothing we long for at the core of our souls comes without effort.

Pursuing discomfort will always land us back in the status quo. Rather than weighing risks, opportunities, and decisions with genuine thoughtfulness,—looking at the pros and cons—we immediately choose the comfortable path. Even when it's destructive toward ourselves and our goals. A low tolerance for discomfort guarantees we'll continue the cycles we've been on rather than doing something new. Newness, or change, is usually less comfortable than the norm, even if that is what we're trying to escape.

I see the capacity for discomfort exemplified in my heroes and role models. I train many high-level executives with unthinkable schedules and enormous pressure on their shoulders. I'm always shocked that with their minimal free time, they're not watching television or going to the beach. Instead, they're in a gym with me, sweating and struggling even more than they already were outside the gym. But that's the thing I needed to understand. The men I chose as my role models aren't *trying* to make it easier on themselves. They do not live in pursuit of comfort; they live in the quest of wholeness. That's why instead of working overtime or watching television, they invest in something momentarily uncomfortable, which ultimately results in energy, strength, and better sleep. They pursue discomfort in the short term to strategically care for themselves, protect themselves from burnout, and propel themselves toward their purpose for the duration.

Ultimately, this is what derails us from facing our fight. We're not derailed by trying something and failing. A catastrophic blowout does not throw us off. Rather, we squirm away from the threat of discomfort. The discomfort of doing something new and hanging in there while we adjust to the exposed feelings it brings. The discomfort of knowing you *could* fail if you keep going. The discomfort of unfamiliarity and an unknown future we can't control. No,

> No, it's not failure that derails us; we're derailed by discomfort before we even have the chance to fail.

it's not failure that derails us; we're derailed by discomfort before we even have the chance to fail.

First and foremost, we commit to winning our fight by acknowledging that discomfort will come and bracing ourselves in preparation for it. Let's prepare for the inevitable pain before entering raw areas of our lives. Otherwise, it'll be like getting caught off guard by a wave in the ocean. It can knock the wind out of us, sweep us off our stable ground, and place us two steps back from where we started. However, we do not need to be caught off guard. When we know the wave is coming, we can adjust our stance. We can counter our fear of it by diving in head-first. We can develop habits and implement accountability systems that help us stay standing when the wave of discomfort hits.

4

HOW TO WIN WHEN YOUR OPPONENT IS YOU

To be yourself in a world that is constantly trying to make you something else is the greatest accomplishment.
—RALPH WALDO EMERSON

Before my world came crashing down around me during my first year of marriage, I didn't think I was avoiding anything! I was burning the candle at both ends, making every effort to be on the right track. However, I lacked the emotional awareness to see that I was avoiding deeper wounds, fears, and areas of dissonance under the surface. My avoidance only served to push those root issues further out of sight.

Often, we run without even realizing it. When it comes to wounds, disappointments, or losses from the past, we may say things like this:

"There's no reason to dredge up the past. It'll only make it worse."

"I've moved on."

"I don't want to make her feel bad."

"He probably won't remember what happened, anyway."

"I'm over it."

Sometimes, these are valid. Occasionally, we've already processed through an issue, and it's not productive to dive back into it in this season. Other times, we're not ready to reopen an event—meaning, to do so would be unproductive and overwhelming because we don't have the capacity or tools to process it. However, phrases like these often ring empty, even if we really believe them in the moment.

To commit to our fight, we must understand avoidance to recognize it in ourselves, even when it's not immediately apparent.

➤ RECOGNIZING HOW WE RUN

While we may not be consciously aware of what discomfort we're avoiding, some signs can point us in the right direction.

1. Apathy

When events or emotions from our past are too overwhelming to handle, we can numb ourselves to them.

Whenever people asked about my past, I'd say, "I don't think about that stuff—I'm over it." Well into my twenties, I was still behaving like the boy who failed his math test and said, "I don't care. I didn't even try." I was only covering it with a mask of apathy because caring—or admitting I cared—opened me to the possibility of being hurt, experiencing failure, and being judged.

It's highly vulnerable to care and takes a lot of emotional energy. But, if we want to face our fight, we have to meet it and be open to looking at what happened to us in our past. When we say, "I don't even miss my brother," "I'm over what she did to me," "My heritage doesn't affect me," "I've moved on," and other dismissive comments, we're putting up a wall to defend ourselves rather than making statements of healing. All those feelings are strategies you've learned to run from your fight. But, if you're reading this book, I'm guessing that you've realized it's time to quit running. It's time to acknowledge your feelings and your past's impact on you. And owning the pain in your past is an essential first step in that journey.

2. Overreaction

While apathy is an underreaction that gives us away, overreaction can also indicate something deeper. When we are running from the fight, we are likely to get triggered. Certain things will strike a nerve. We will suddenly feel intense emotions over something objectively small—a miscommunication, making a minor mistake, being cut off on the freeway, or our partner not calling us back. Those close to us become confused by our reactions, feeling as if they're walking over a minefield, unable to tell which step will cause an explosion. We may not even understand our response ourselves, why something bothered or affected us as much as it did.

This strong emotional response is evidence that there's something deeper under the surface we haven't yet resolved. Our brain is going into "panic mode" because the current situation has brought up an unresolved fear, even in some indirect way. We can't simply *will* ourselves not to react this way. To change this reaction, we must press into the discomfort of the buried issues behind this reaction and address it from the root.

3. Distraction

Distractions come in many forms, and they seem innocent enough. Not to mention they're easier to come by than ever before. We have a million apps at our fingertips. Television series, movies, social media, relationships, good food, and self-care can inspire, refresh, and nourish us. Innocent enough, right?

While distractions can be helpful to let our minds rest a bit, the trouble comes when these distractions hinder our processing and connection with ourselves and the world around us. We can easily use any of these as an "out" to avoid having a needed conversation, sitting with our thoughts, resolving a conflict, creating a better habit, or investing in our priorities. Unable to sit alone with our thoughts, we can turn to hours on hours of scrolling instead of resting in our free time. Binge-watching instead of working or seeing friends can even evolve into habits of drinking, binge eating, and using sex or drugs to cope with an unnamable internal ache. Suppose we cannot control these impulses and sit alone without spiraling. In that case, we must recognize we're using these forms of entertainment or pleasure as a crutch to avoid discomfort.

Apathy, overreaction, distraction, and other coping strategies may help in the moment but ultimately keep us from growth. Rather than healing, these coping mechanisms push the wounds deeper—to a place where we can't even feel them. But deep beneath the surface, they continue to fester and grow. The only way to heal them is to become aware of how we're running and what we're running from.

Do you resonate with any of these? Have you noticed yourself feeling apathetic toward something—even if you'd like to feel sad, mad, etc., you just can't? Does your brain latch onto something small and fall into a downward spiral outside your control? Which distractions do you have the hardest time resisting? Do you see any other patterns of avoidance? When we identify how we run, we can move closer to the root of these habits and begin unraveling them from the source.

RUNNING AS A TRAUMA RESPONSE

Sometimes, we're not just ignoring the problem; our brains are hiding memories that are too painful to face. This means our brains can literally *forget* something traumatic as a form of temporary self-protection.

Yet the hidden memory still impacts us without our awareness. "Eventually those suppressed memories can cause debilitating psychological problems, such as anxiety, depression, post-traumatic stress disorder, or dissociative disorders," according to Northwestern's Feinberg School of Medicine[1]. At some point, we must remember the past to heal fully. That often can only be done in therapy, as retrieving a lost memory requires specific strategies.

While I never completely forgot the day of the gunshots, my brain did spend a long time blurring the details so I wouldn't have to remember the specifics. I did recall all the details in a therapy session years later, as I've written in this book. While this was extremely difficult, it finally allowed me to grieve the experience and understand what happened from an adult lens. Once I stopped running and faced this memory, I could finally begin healing from it.

➤ TRAINING OURSELVES OUT OF AVOIDANCE

As an extension of facing discomfort, we commit to winning our fight by unraveling our avoidance habits.

Do you ever find yourself in one of those moments when the distraction fails? Your plans get canceled, and you have nothing to do. You're driving, but your AUX cord broke, or your Bluetooth won't connect. You have to wait in line, but your phone is dead. You're on an airplane, and you forgot to download your music or show. You're on a trip, and there's no wifi. For even a few moments, you're forced to sit alone, in silence, with your thoughts. We can't always control where they go! Our thoughts may replay scenarios from earlier in the day, tense moments, or interactions you could have handled differently. Perhaps you find yourself mulling over worst-case scenarios, anxieties about the future, or the tasks weighing on you. This space is a breeding ground for unproductive overthinking and catastrophizing. It can feel extremely overwhelming and unpleasant if we're not used to this feeling and don't know how to handle it.

PATTERNS OF AVOIDING DISCOMFORT

> ➤ According to workplace resource startup Bravely, 70% of employees avoid difficult conversations with their boss, colleagues, and direct reports.[2]

> ➤ According to Pew Research Center, for people between the ages of 18 and 29, nearly 93% reported using their phone to avoid boredom or the people around them.[3]

> ➤ A survey of more than 24,000 adults across 23 countries showed that 42% of people go to the movies as frequently as possible to escape from reality.[4]

While these moments can feel overwhelming, there is a unique opportunity available to us here. In moments like this, we uncover the truth: the discomfort will not hurt us. We think it will hurt us because when we avoid discomfort at all costs, we develop something called "discomfort anxiety." It convinces us discomfort will put us in danger. In reality, the opposite is true. Avoidance puts us in danger—physically, relationally, emotionally, and spiritually. This avoidance creates self-inflicted pain, much worse than discomfort. This self-sabotage is the cause of so much suffering in our lives. However, we can unravel this habit.

Years ago, I decided that I no longer wanted my life dictated by what's comfortable or uncomfortable. When I did, I learned something critical. In the same way that we train the muscles in our body to lift more, we can train our minds to handle more discomfort with less and less anxiety.

By intentionally *practicing* discomfort, we can turn our habit of avoiding it into a habit of facing it. In doing so, we expand our tolerance for it. Once I recognized some key areas where I was avoiding discomfort, I chose ways of practicing discomfort. That pointed me toward the growth I had been missing. Here are a few of the ways I have chosen to expand my tolerance for discomfort in recent years:

> Began going to therapy to work on my marriage and be a better father for my kids
> Chose a close group of men to share all parts of my life with, including marital struggles, bank statements, big decisions, etc.
> Started waking up at 3:30 a.m. so my work time wouldn't cut into time with my family
> Hired a running coach for myself (I hate running)
> Started regularly taking ice baths
> Started learning to rest and delegating to my team

Additionally, you'll read more examples in the following chapters. It is the thread throughout every story of transformation in this book. Each of these actions committed me to my fight more deeply. My actions declared that my health, growth, and relationships were worth the discomfort. The more I pursued things that made me uncomfortable, the more confidence I built in my ability to handle that discomfort. I became less and less afraid of it as I realized it couldn't hurt me. Every area of my life has grown significantly as a result.

TOOL FOR MOMENTS WITHOUT DISTRACTION

How should we respond when there are no distractions or when we try to set them aside?

1. Take a deep breath and count to 10.
2. Express gratitude: What was one bright spot in your day today?
3. Identify your feelings: How am I feeling? What do I need?
4. What's important today?
5. How can I focus on that rather than getting caught up in distractions?

While this practice may feel uncomfortable, it will anchor you back in the present moment so you can make decisions out of intentionality rather than omission.

I want to clarify that we don't press into discomfort just for its own sake. We don't get extra points just for suffering without a cause. It is not about proving our-selves or tolerating any form of mistreatment. Not to mention, discomfort doesn't always mean taking action. Sometimes, we're on the road to burnout, and we must embrace discomfort by learning to rest and take care of ourselves. When I say to embrace discomfort, I'm talking about the discomfort that comes with growing—when the pursuit of your goals leads you to do what you've never done before. It's when growing requires the risk of failure, and there's no way around it. I embrace discomfort for my marriage and family. I embrace discomfort for my dreams.

When we do embrace growth-oriented discomfort, we receive unparalleled clarity. We realize what we were afraid of isn't that scary. It empowers us; we're ready for the next challenge. We realize discomfort will not kill us, but that once we are through it, we are closer to being who we want to be.

Whenever I think about the day Diana and I were sup-posed to see the movie, there is one thought that speaks loudest: I am so grateful for that meltdown, and that it shook me out of my cycles of avoidance, even though it was uncomfortable. When I look at my life now, I realize how minuscule the cost that discomfort was for what I have gained.

5

THE WINNER'S UNEXPECTED SUPERPOWER

Without leaps of imagination or dreaming,
we lose the excitement of possibilities.
Dreaming, after all, is a form of planning.

—GLORIA STEINEM

Committing to winning means embracing the discomfort of growth and undoing our avoidance habits. But this is extremely difficult to do. We need something that makes it worth it. In other words, we need a vision of what we're fighting for. To fully commit to winning, we need a clear picture of what we want to win. It may be more powerful than we think. Let me tell you a story.

One of my favorite childhood memories started the first year we spent the holidays without my dad. I was eleven, and my little brother was six. Our dad had recently moved out, and as Christmas grew nearer, there was no sign we would celebrate it as usual. My brother and I cautiously approached the holiday, unsure of what to expect. While we could somewhat ignore the loss in day-to-day life, the consistent rhythms of the holiday made our change this year feel glaring.

The three of us got up early, ate breakfast, opened gifts, and stared at each other. We would not go to my uncle's house this year, and a lonely day loomed before us.

Then our mom had an idea.

"Wait!" she stopped us from retreating to our rooms. She grabbed her keys from the wooden table. "Grab your jackets. We're going out!"

My brother and I looked at each other with intrigue. *Where were we going?*

We ran down the driveway through the crisp air and the three of us piled into our mom's white station wagon. Our eyes grew wide as we screeched to a stop in the McDonald's drive-through.

> To fully commit to winning, we need a clear picture of what we want to win.

The tinny voice in the box asked if we were ready to order.

"We're getting *fast food*?!" It was a novelty in our home. This was a special occasion indeed.

Our paper bags came filled with burgers, fries cascading out of the little red cartons, and tall sodas. We giggled as we pulled away, like we were doing something rebellious, eating McDonald's on Christmas.

Our jaws dropped again when we pulled up in front of the movie theatre, of all places. Weren't you legally obligated to spend all of Christmas inside your Auntie's stuffy old home, making small talk with your grandma about your favorite subject in school? We sat in the movie theatre and ate our McDonald's, feeling like three giggling children together.

My mom always tried to shield us from the acknowledgment that our family unit was falling apart. "See? We can still have good times together!" And her smile convinced us as we sipped our forbidden bubbly sodas. And we did have a great time. We continued this tradition every year. It was precious to us. It represented how, on the worst Christmas of our lives, we banded together with french fries and laughed. We were all we had, and we made that enough.

At age thirty-five, this is still one of my favorite childhood memories. However, it didn't eliminate the pain of our fractured family. As a teen, I remember times when we'd go out to eat, and at another table, I'd see a mom, dad, and their kids all bickering around the table. My face would burn with envy. I saw this stability, this wholeness that I would never have, and I'd have to look away.

I wondered if I would ever have a family like that when I grew up. It seemed like some people were destined to have a normal life, and I was not one of those people. But I wanted that wholeness so badly. When I closed my eyes, I imagined the family again, but I was the dad. In my mind, I was holding my wife's hand, our kids were around the table, and we were all together.

While I struggled to believe it could become my story, I still imagined it, and I painted in my mind what didn't exist in my real life. These mental pictures were vivid, and I pictured taking my family to the zoo, tucking my kids in bed at night, going on trips together.

Even after Diana and I got married, I still struggled to believe we could have a regular, whole family. Both from families of divorce and dysfunction, we had much to learn and unlearn about how a family should operate. At times, we felt hopelessly broken. The discomfort of wading through the dark in this area was so palpable. We could have stuffed our problems, kept them to ourselves, and allowed our marriage to fall apart slowly, as so many do. However, something continued to drive me through these moments of despair.

The source of that hope was this vision I had been nurturing since my teen years—this image that one day my family would be one of wholeness. It was too deep into my mind; I couldn't let it go. Despite our history and our latest fight, I felt strangely prepared for this vision to come to pass.

▶ THE POWER OF VISUALIZATION

Unbeknownst to me, I had intuitively discovered a vital tool in the process of transformation: visualizing one's success.

Visualization means forming a mental image of something, even when—especially when—that thing is not visible to you. We do this all the time, whether we intend to or not. When we're afraid, we often vividly visualize what could go wrong. We paint it in extreme detail—exactly how it would look, sound, feel, taste, or smell. But how often do we visualize what could go right? How often do we permit ourselves to paint a vivid mental picture of what our own success could look, sound, feel, taste, and smell like?

This act of imagination is our superpower as humans—arguably the key ability that separates our species from others. Other animals can communicate, create tools, and cooperate on a large scale. However, we are the only species that can build scenarios in our minds that don't yet exist. We can tell stories, picture future situations, imagine others' experiences, contemplate potential explanations, plan how to teach, and reflect on moral dilemmas. And yet, do we take advantage of this power as often as we can?

Our skill for scenario-building explodes at age two. I see this constantly in my three young kids. Their minds are teeming with people, places, animals, inventions—entire worlds that don't exist! Their imaginations know no limits. We only gain these limits through our life experiences that teach us—sometimes erroneously—what's possible and what's not.

However, imagination is not just child's play. Recent studies have shed light on the practical power of imagination in our ability to achieve goals. One study monitored the brain patterns of weightlifters when lifting hundreds of pounds compared to just imagining lifting hundreds of pounds. The brain patterns activated in both cases were nearly the same!

In some cases, these mental practices have proven to be almost as effective, even in building physical strength. Guang Yue, an exercise psychologist from Cleveland Clinic Foundation in Ohio, conducted a study having everyday people do finger strength exercises.[5] One group performed physical exercises spreading and contracting their fingers while the other performed the workouts solely in their heads. In the group that did physical exercises, finger abduction strength increased by fifty-three percent. But the group who only did "mental contractions" increased finger abduction strength by thirty-five percent—without even moving their fingers! When tested again four weeks after the training ended, some in the mental exercise category even increased to forty percent. That shows that our mind and imagination have far more power over our real-life progress than we might expect.[6]

THE HISTORY OF VISUALIZATION

This form of "mental practice" is not a recent discovery. It has been popular since the 1970s when the Soviets used it in sports competitions. Countless athletes like Tiger Woods, Jack Nicklaus, and Muhammad Ali practice their sport by using highly detailed mental imagery. I use it consistently when training clients and athletes. Brain studies now show that this mental rehearsal produces the same mental instructions as performing the action. As a result, these practices impact motor control, attention, perception, planning, memory, motivation, and self-efficacy. They improve motor performance and increase states of flow, preparing us to actualize what's in our minds.[7]

Visualization requires us to reignite the skill of imagination that we often lose as adults. It relights in me as I see it forming in my children, who are all under six years old as I write this. The more they develop their imaginations, the fewer limits exist for them. Even as toddlers, they are capable of imagining realities that do not physically exist yet in the world. Isn't that wild? Imagination is a powerful force that manifests the future. We would not have cars, planes, the internet, or most of the things we consider necessities today if it were not for the power of imagining a reality beyond the one that exists. Imagination spurs our hope to see victory even before the victory has been won.

➤ VISUALIZING THE FIGHT

The practice of visualization is critical for us as we face the fight in our lives. It answers the question: for what are you training? It helps us paint a clear vision we can hold onto when we feel discouraged. You need to see yourself up on that podium. You need to vividly imagine what that win will feel like. The one you never thought you could have. The win you believed was only reserved for others. This mental image fuels our sense of purpose and tenacity behind the tedious, strenuous repetition required to change our lives.

As we imagine ourselves facing our fight, our brain prepares us to do so. We process what obstacles may be present and mentally work through how we will navigate them. We imagine consequences that might occur and how we will cope if they do. We anticipate what temptations will be present and rehearse how we will overcome them. Our brain builds the muscles to complete these actions in real life through this process.

Visualization represents a hope that our story can change. As we imagine ourselves winning the fight, we develop greater confidence and familiarity with seeing ourselves in this position. That hope is the first step toward making the change a reality. Imagine:

> Being in a hospital in a cast but you are healed and walking again

> Being in a position where you are barely making rent but then being handed the keys to the new house you just bought

> Currently taking the bus and getting into your car for the first time

> Growing up in a turbulent family situation but one day having your own partner, children, and healthy family

> Being in jail and holding your kid at their fifteenth birthday party after missing five years of their life

These powerful mental images can't actualize reality on their own. Still, they position us and prepare us, drastically increasing the odds of these things happening.

Visualization doesn't operate by magic; it's effective because of the change it works in us. Visualizing moves us closer to victory

Visualization represents a hope that our story can change.

because it increases our awareness of what *could be*. It increases our envy of that life. It increases our motivation— but also our sense that that really could be our life. Our desire for that victory grows as the "obstacles" we've always assumed grow smaller. Our circumstances may remain the same, but our motivation and sense of self-efficacy significantly improve our ability to win our fight.

ACTION PLAN:
VISUALIZE YOUR VICTORY

1. What three areas of your life do you most want to see transformed? Example: Family, career, time management, creativity, friendships, marriage, parenting?
2. Ten years from now, what would victory look like in these three areas?
   a. Write this in vivid detail, as if it were a scene in a movie. Use all five senses to describe it, if you can (what would it look, sound, smell, taste, and feel like)?

STRATEGY TWO:

CLAIM YOUR POWER

CLAIM YOUR POWER

6

THE MINDSETS THAT TAKE OUR POWER

If you think tough men are dangerous, wait until you see what weak men are capable of.

—JORDAN PETERSON

It was my freshman year of college, and I participated in a car wash fundraiser with my university. We started early in the morning. By afternoon, the sun was high overhead, and it was so hot the soap was almost drying before we could rinse it. Still, a steady stream of cars kept rolling in, tossing a five-, ten-, or twenty-dollar bill to the sophomore attendant at the entrance.

Despite the heat, I was having a good time because I got to wash beside one of my best friends, Jeremy. He didn't go to the university but frequented service events like this one. He'd gone to jail as a juvenile and needed to rack up service hours as a requirement now that he was out. That was how we first met—at an event like this—even though he was six years older than me.

Being so much older, Jeremy filled a long-desired big brother role for me. Whether or not he was exactly qualified for the position, he took it seriously, trying to make sure I didn't repeat his mistakes. Jeremy would pick me up from school and take me to the gym—he was the first one who got me into fitness—and I latched onto him. While he was fun to be around, he also felt consistent and safe.

Jeremy was notorious for joking around, and laughter followed him, even to a sweaty mid-summer car wash. We kept our spirits high and avoided heat stroke with some good-natured splashing and sponge-tossing.

Just as I sent a drippy sponge flying over the top of an older, mid-sized Lexus, I felt my shirt collar catch around my neck. My body spun around involuntarily. Within a second, I was nose-to-nose with a middle-aged man I had never seen before. He was taller than me, with graying hair and little brown age spots dotting his temples.

He gripped my collar tightly and snarled, "Stop f*cking around and wash my damn car."

I shook myself loose and looked at him, stunned. *What just happened?* Obviously, he thought I wasn't putting in the elbow grease his five-dollar donation merited. It only took a moment before my anger caught up. My first instinct was to hit him. I was going to knock him out. But even in the rage of that moment, I was aware enough to know that if I sent this older man to the ground, the carwash would be over. I would get into a load of trouble. I glared at him and turned back to washing his car, silently stewing until all the vehicles were clean, keeping my eyes down and ignoring everything else.

The day was winding down. Some volunteers were already cracking open the grocery store cupcakes someone had brought. My own car was one of the last few left. As I dropped my five dollars in the donation bucket, I turned around to see my friend Jeremy rocket a pink frosted cupcake into my windshield. Everyone laughed—it was about to be washed anyway. No harm done, right?

> I craved control, but not because I wanted to dominate others. I desired control in response to a deep-seated fear from my early wound.

I blew up at him. I started screaming at the top of my lungs, cussing him out. My best friend! He was dumbfounded. He had never seen me like this, and everyone watched in horror. I wanted to hit him, but I got in my car and slammed the door. I stomped on the gas, and my brakes screeched as I left the parking lot, pink frosting dripping down the glass.

I drove straight home. When I got there, I felt horrible and sick to my stomach. I immediately called Jeremy to apologize.

"I screwed up, man. I'm so sorry. I have no idea why I did that. You didn't deserve that."

He said it was cool, but our friendship never recovered.

➤ FALSE ATTEMPTS TO CLAIM OUR POWER

I learned early on that anger was a way of exerting power. From my father to this man at the carwash, the angriest man in the room was always in control.

I craved control, but not because I wanted to dominate others. I desired control in response to a deep-seated fear from my early wound. I felt weak and helpless when I watched my dad nearly take my mom's life that day. I never wanted to feel that weak and vulnerable again in my life. The memory was so deeply etched into my brain that I lived in fear of it, even when I wasn't consciously thinking about it. Therefore, I always needed to have the upper hand. If I couldn't come out on top, I panicked because the self-defense instinct in my brain told me I wasn't safe. It activated my fear response. Between fight, flight, and freeze, I fought. In that way, I used anger as my shield and offense as my defense.

The problem was that while my anger gave me a temporary sense of control, I could not control the anger itself. As I grew into adulthood, I learned to tame this intense emotion where it wasn't socially acceptable. But it continued to show up in my closest relationships—namely, my marriage.

Diana and I worked long hours with conflicting schedules in our first married year, and we ran into conflict often. We constantly misunderstood each other, snapping reactively out of exhaustion and lacking quality time to bond and understand each other. When Diana would bring this to my attention, I'd often react with anger, like my father. I'd yell, storm out, and blame her, ultimately pushing my wife further from me. It was not the type of marriage I wanted, but I didn't know who I could talk to about it for fear of being judged when I already felt bad enough.

Ultimately, this emotional reaction was an attempt to reclaim the power I felt I had lost as a child. Still, it was not an effective way of doing so. This strategy convinced my brain I was safe at the moment, but in reality, it did not make me any safer. It only served to damage my closest relationships. It also increased my fear that I'd become exactly like my dad. I felt conflicted about becoming a man who could feel safe and in control without dominating or hurting others.

> The problem was that while my anger gave me a temporary sense of control, I could not control the anger itself.

Maybe you can relate to my story about losing my temper. Okay, maybe you didn't cuss someone out at a university car wash or yell when you got upset. But can you think of a time in your life when you were stressed, sad, disappointed, or tired, so you snapped at someone who didn't deserve it? You replied a little too harshly. Responded with irritation, but it wasn't about them. You had emotions rattling inside you without an outlet, so they found one. And it wasn't your proudest moment. Maybe it was hurtful toward someone you cared about, or you ruined a stranger's day. Maybe you lost a friend, like me. It wasn't until years later that I began to understand the roots of this complex emotion and unravel its hold on my life.

➤ MASCULINITY AND EMOTIONAL INTELLIGENCE

I know many men who think they are "just not emotional." Usually, this means they don't cry at the sad Super Bowl commercials—the ones with the dogs, the horses, the older men who learn to love again. It also may mean they go through their day regularly without thinking about their emotions or spending long hours talking about them, like their "inner world" is a place they may visit occasionally. Still, they can't get there without prompting.

Some resign to the idea that women are just better at understanding emotions. However, no neurological evidence supports the dichotomy that women are emotional and men are logical. Whether we consider ourselves emotional or not, we all have emotions because we're human. We run through many emotions in a day, whether we are aware of them or know how to put language to them.

While some may view being less emotional as a personality trait, it's helpful to look at our experience and how it fits into the larger picture. In the last fifteen years, the American Psychological Association has been compiling research from decades past to understand the struggles of men. Men were the sole focus of psychological research until the 1960s. With all that history invested into men's care, shouldn't men be pretty well off? You'd think. Yet men still commit ninety percent of homicides and represent seventy-seven percent of homicide victims. Men are three and a half times more likely to die by suicide, and their life expectancy is almost five years shorter than women's. Boys are more likely to be diagnosed with ADHD and face harsher punishments in school. With so much research and effort toward men's wellbeing, why is there still so much struggle?

To address these alarming statistics, researchers studied men's experiences more closely. From their research, one finding became abundantly clear across the board: "Traditional masculinity [otherwise known as toxic masculinity]—marked by stoicism, competitiveness, dominance, and aggression—is, on the whole, harmful."

Men raised with this understanding of masculinity were less likely to admit vulnerability, seek psychological help, seek preventative health care, or even eat vegetables! They were more apt to show risky behavior, drink heavily, use tobacco, and encourage others to do the same.[8] So many of us were raised with this definition of masculinity, and the results are showing it has not served us well.

> No neurological evidence supports the dichotomy that women are emotional and men are logical. Whether we consider ourselves emotional or not, we all have emotions because we're human.

To clarify, masculinity itself is not the problem. It's not wrong to embrace masculine traits. But when those traits become so exaggerated that they hurt yourself and others, they become toxic. Overall, toxic masculinity teaches men to suck it up, tough it out, come out on top, and don't let them see you sweat. And because men aren't taught to open up, we all think we're alone. It's no wonder we're struggling.

The most damaging and limiting part of toxic masculinity is that it robs us of emotional intelligence. Emotional intelligence is the "capacity to be aware of, control, and express one's emotions, and to handle interpersonal relationships judiciously and empathetically."[9] When we lack this basic skill, we're unable to work through any other issue that arises.

Trust me when I say that I did not learn how to be emotionally intelligent growing up. What emotional intelligence I have was learned as an adult, and I'm continually working on expanding it. My teachers have been men I've carefully chosen who live out their commitment to emotional competency. I've also learned from women like my wife, mother, and other friends, who have patiently given me room to grow, change, and apologize.

When I finally began seeking help, other men's stories of how they struggled validated my own. I began noticing patterns that I later found language for when I finally went to therapy. And I continued developing language for these trends as I coached other young men.

Each of these steps were uncomfortable. Sharing with other men was vulnerable and opened the potential to be rejected, misunderstood, or alienated. I risked having someone say, "What's wrong with you?" and sinking me deeper into the shame I already felt. Therapy was uncomfortable, sitting down in a setting and type of relationship that was utterly foreign to me. Going to therapy put me at complete odds with the cultural norms of my family and heritage. I replayed back through many of my most difficult memories. Yet the growth I received from these uncomfortable experiences was unparalleled.

While toxic masculinity touts power and control, it leaves men ultimately powerless. As we train for our fight, a lack of emotional awareness leaves us swinging in the dark. As men, we must challenge ourselves to push past the discomfort of exploring our inner world. Whether it's a place we naturally live in, constantly conscious of our thoughts and feelings,

> As men, we must challenge ourselves to push past the discomfort of exploring our inner world.

or a place we visit when prompted (or forced). If we avoid, we will continue claiming power in ways that disempower us and hurt those around us.

7

THE DANGER OF UNCLAIMED EMOTIONS

Many of us live inhuman lives because we believe inhuman rules like 'don't be sad,' 'it's bad to be angry,' or, 'you're weak if you're afraid.'

—PETER SCAZZERO

To authentically reclaim power in our fight, we must study our internal world and understand the existing patterns. Only then can we make an intentional effort to rewire our reaction and take control of how we let our past and present affect us.

In my family, I was always "the angry brother." When I felt something negative, anger was the easiest emotion to access. When I was sad, I got angry. When I was disappointed, I got angry. It was the closest emotion to the surface, the most accessible feeling to express. The only way I knew how to release emotion was to explode.

While not everyone struggles with anger, we all tend to have a "knee-jerk" emotion. This emotion comes as our first instinct when we become upset or afraid. Besides anger, another example of this might be sadness. Someone may cry whether they're angry, overwhelmed, shocked, or worried. For others, the easiest emotion to access may be apathy. People who feel this way may tend to withdraw, whether they're sad, hurt, nervous, etc. For example, when my little brother got upset, he might sulk, become quiet, and go to his room. He never exploded as I did. If anything, he'd collapse in on himself, falling deep into his private world, withdrawing until it felt like he wasn't even there.

A combination of factors causes our knee-jerk: a significant wound in our past, our upbringing, and our unique disposition.

My most significant childhood wound was closely related to aggression and power dominance. My father physically dominated my mother with anger and aggression. My grandpa and uncle then dominated him by overpowering him through aggressiveness and strength. The idea I internalized was not that anger was wrong but that you had to be angrier to win. However, not everyone's core wound relates to aggression and power. Others may relate more to needing to be perfect, avoiding shame, being abandoned, etc. These may yield a different result, teaching a young brain to protect itself differently.

THE ROLE OF CHILDHOOD TRAUMA IN OUR EMOTIONAL LIFE

While I struggled for years with my tension between fear and anger, I now recognize this is a prevalent feeling for those who have experienced trauma, especially in childhood and within the family unit. In 2010, the National Coalition Against Domestic Violence reported that one in fifteen children was exposed to cases of intimate partner violence, with one in three children experiencing acts of violence themselves. Typical responses include going into a state of perpetual anxiety, Post-Traumatic Stress Disorder, somatic symptoms, aggressive behavior, and becoming physically abusive. In the long term, kids who experience domestic trauma often grow into adults who suffer from depression and health issues and continue the abusive patterns in their adult relationships.[10]

When we experience this type of existential fear early on, our brains go into self-defense mode: fight, flight, or freeze. This is certainly one explanation for why children who experience domestic trauma can develop aggressive behavior early on and continue abusive patterns in their adult associations. We don't develop anger because we want to be angry; we develop anger because it's one of our brain's most basic ways to protect ourselves.

It tries to protect us from physical harm. But it also attempts to protect us from confronting the deeper emotions like fear, hurt, disappointment, shame, or sadness. Yet when we fail to address these more profound emotions, we forfeit control over where they lead us and what trajectory they set our lives on.

As for my upbringing, the anger felt like something I inherited rather than chose—the way you inherit your mom's nose or use the same mannerisms as your dad. While my dad wasn't very emotionally expressive, the rare times he did show emotion, it was often in the form of anger. And this was the most acceptable emotion for us to offer as boys in the household. More vulnerable, soft emotions like sadness, insecurity, doubt, or fear seemed more forbidden than anger, even though they'd likely have been less destructive. For other families, perhaps every emotion besides anger was acceptable, so the offense was left brewing without an outlet, simmering in other displays like irritation, withdraw, stress, or pretending.

> While not everyone struggles with anger, we all tend to have a "knee-jerk" emotion. This emotion comes as our first instinct when we become upset or afraid.

Lastly, our knee-jerk emotional reaction also differs depending on our disposition. Whether it's our genes, birth order, or something woven into the fabric of who we are, we each carry our unique personalities. Two people in identical situations may react and try to protect themselves differently. Perhaps my brother would have reacted more like me if he was older and I was younger, since my reaction was shaped by his looking up to me. We can't know for sure. All we can do is work to understand our reactions.

Regardless of our wounds, upbringing, or disposition, no knee-jerk emotion is good or bad—it simply *is*. Some may be flashier than others, but none is better or worse. Anger can have painful, irreversible effects, but so can withdrawing. Unbridled anxiety or sadness can damage relationships as well. The problem is not which emotion we happen to be able to access most easily. That is somewhat arbitrary, primarily formed in us outside of our control. Whatever the emotion, our task remains the same; we must learn how to control our emotions rather than being controlled by them.

➤ BUILDING EMOTIONAL VOCABULARY

If we can't name it, we can't claim it. If we can't claim it, we can't control it.

That is an excellent rule of thumb with emotions. That is the problem when we oversimplify what we're feeling, relying on anger, sadness, or withdrawing and not naming it at all. We will always be controlled by our emotions when we cannot articulate them. Yes, perhaps we are angry. But beneath that anger, we feel hurt. Humiliated. Indignant. Yes, maybe we are anxious. But beneath that anxiety, we feel grieved. Out of control. Excluded. Yes, we might be sad. But beneath that sadness, we feel disrespected. Insignificant. Jealous. We often find several more complex feelings at play if we mine that one emotion to see what lies beneath it.

Some men I've worked with avoid this process because they fear it'll only worsen things. However, emotions still exist even when we refuse to recognize them. Being unaware of them also doesn't mean we're not affected by them—they still influence our relationships, habits, and decisions beneath our consciousness. In fact, they have far more power over us in their unrecognized state, controlling our life from behind the scenes.

While identifying these more specific feelings may not be pleasant, they are helpful to us. The first emotion we feel is often just the tip of the iceberg. But when we can identify what emotions lie beneath, we can begin to work through them in pro-

> If we can't name it, we can't claim it. If we can't claim it, we can't control it.

ductive ways that allow us to heal and control them better in the future.

Only years later could I understand why I acted the way I did at the car wash—I could identify the emotions that existed beneath my anger. When that man grabbed me by the collar, I felt insecure, disrespected, and hurt. A boundary was crossed, and no one else did anything about it or spoke up for me, making me feel insignificant and betrayed. I felt humiliated that I had to keep washing his car after that. I felt sad and afraid. I was able to contain myself and not take it out on this man, but all those emotions still raged inside me.

Feeling unsafe and out of control, my brain activated my "fight response" to try and regain my sense of control, even in an irrational way. So, when my best friend threw the cupcake, I misdirected that aggression toward him. I wish I could have known then what I know now. I could have calmed down long enough to tell him what I felt and recognize that he was in my corner. It could have saved our friendship.

When we men investigate our emotions, we are not acting un-masculine. Rather, we are tapping into how masculinity is supposed to look. In fact, ignoring our emotions and letting them control our lives without us knowing it is un-masculine. It is every man's (and every person's) responsibility to investigate and manage their emotions. When we suppress or lack intentionality with our feelings, we forfeit the fight for our growth.

➤ THE FEELINGS WHEEL

One of the tools I've gained over the last several years is the Feelings Wheel.[11] In the center of the wheel are the broadest emotions, often the easiest to identify first.

Those emotions get more specific as the circle moves out into the second layer. In the outermost layer, the emotions' titles get even more specific.

To use this tool, start by identifying the center emotions you resonate with. Then, move outward from there, choosing which of the more specific emotions accurately describes how you feel.

The Feelings Wheel is an extremely helpful tool to use in a variety of scenarios. I often use this when journaling or reflecting on my own to aid my internal processing of a situation or a day. Even if nothing particularly upsetting happened, this practice helps me slow down and see if I overlooked any feelings. For example, irritation towards a co-worker might come up later if I don't acknowledge and work through it. I also use this with my wife as we communicate through conflict and determine how to help one another. I use a simplified version with my kids to help them develop the emotional intelligence I lacked at their age. It's also helpful with my friends, staff, and clients as we work through any conflict between us or process other issues occurring in their lives.

FEELINGS WHEEL

Ultimately, placing names on our emotions is uncomfortable for multiple reasons. Perhaps the biggest is that naming an emotion can make it feel all the more real. Perhaps you're also working through voices from family members telling you to keep it inside you. Maybe you don't want to feel like a burden on others, or like you're being "too dramatic." I understand this feeling.

Sometimes, when I try to articulate how something made me feel, I immediately hear a self-critical voice in my mind saying I'm making a big deal out of it, and I need to get over it and let it go. However, I've realized over time that this voice in my head is not championing my growth. The voice in my head is trying to protect me, wants me to play it safe, and avoid conflict and embarrassment. While its intentions may be good, it doesn't know best. And listening to that voice ultimately abdicates my power rather than claiming it.

8

THE METHODS OF EMOTIONAL MASTERY

*The decisions you make today will determine
the stories you tell tomorrow.*

—CRAIG GROESCHEL

Recently, Diana and I took our kids to Disneyland. We waited in line for the tram with a stroller and three children in the sweltering heat. Suddenly, this younger couple walked right in front of us, cutting in line without asking.

"They just cut us!" Diana whisper-yelled in my ear, glaring at the two.

"Yeah, I saw that," I replied casually.

Diana blinked at me. "Aren't you going to do something about it? Five years ago, you'd have been fighting these people!"

I laughed a little. I had struggled with anger for almost our entire relationship and marriage. Now being cut in the tram line at Disney, Diana was almost mad at me for *not* being upset with this rude couple.

But the truth is, she was right. Previously, I'd have called them out and confronted them. I'd have raised my voice and told them how selfish it was, and I'd have asserted myself and my family back in front of them in line. I'd have claimed I was fighting for my family and fairness. But really, I'd have been wasting my time and energy on something futile.

Now, I had no strong feelings about this couple cutting us. Why didn't I feel angry?

This event is a prime example of where my language falls short in describing all the factors that allowed me to exist at that moment, entirely different from how I once was. It wasn't a single realization or technique that mastered my emotions. I had to come to a place where I realized I had a problematic behavior that would ruin my life if I didn't change. I had to accept that my uncontrollable anger was going to destroy my romantic relationship, friendships, and any dreams I had for the future. After that, I continued to ask, "How can I not be this person anymore?" I took one step at a time, making small decisions.

> I realized I had a problematic behavior that would ruin my life if I didn't change.

These decisions included: talking about why I got mad rather than walking away, doing a breathing exercise, apologizing, practicing naming my emotions, sharing with a friend when I had a rough day, reading a book like this one that might enlarge my perspective, and choosing to express my anger in honest prayer. Most of all, I kept taking the next step, developing greater awareness. Then I'd take another.

All those steps over the years accumulated into this one major factor: I became less angry because I was less angry at my dad. Inevitably, it often led back to him when I chose to process my pain. When I took those steps honestly, I wound up unraveling and healing wounds I hadn't intended to deal with. By the time that couple cut us at Disneyland, my acute fears and insecurities had healed. I no longer needed to prove myself as I once did. I had resolved enough of my internal wounds to where I wasn't triggered nearly as easily. I felt safe. I felt secure.

Because I felt safe, my brain could see the situation from a logical, macro perspective. Whether or not we got on this tram, we would get to our destination in relatively the same amount of time. Thinking logically, I could see that our family and stroller may not have fit on this upcoming tram anyways. Yes, what they did was rude, but I could see no real fight here. While I could have given their actions some weight in my emotional state, I did not need to.

As I reflected on this later, I was struck by how much I had grown. I thought about the model I was able to set for my young kids who will face similar situations in life. Facing the fight for emotional health has allowed me to become more of the husband and father I was meant to be.

When I was younger, I mistakenly thought emotional control was all about repression. I needed to keep it inside me, like I did, however briefly, at the car wash when I chose not to hit the man who grabbed me. However, like in that moment and many others, emotional repression led to a later volatile explosion. As a matter of fact, rather than helping me with my anger, emotional repression placed me in my dad's footsteps. I'd seen him angry, but he had never laid a hand on my mom. His volatile explosion resulted from decades of trauma, pain, and stress repressed but never resolved.

While we may repress an emotion at the moment so it doesn't wreak havoc, repression is not a long-term solution. Whatever's inside will come out anyway because we never resolved it. If someone triggers us strongly enough, we cannot repress it at all.

The real way to reclaim our power in the fight is by learning regulation over repression. To regulate our emotions, we must be willing to enter the space where we ask deeper questions. We must be willing to investigate. When we're upset, we may be afraid or hesitant to ask, "Why do I feel this way?" and follow where that trail may lead.

> The real way to reclaim our power in the fight is by learning regulation over repression.

Doing the inner work is difficult and uncomfortable. However, I know that my lack of control in this area has real consequences for those around me, and I want to honor them by being the man I was meant to be. My wife, kids, and friendships are worth it. My community is worth it. Because my relationships will only reach a limited capacity until I address this, I want the depth and healing on the other side.

› TOOLS FOR DE-ESCALATING IN THE MOMENT

Ultimately, the way to freedom lies in understanding and reconciling where the emotion we're feeling comes from in the first place. Our brains are not physically capable of mining our emotions in this way when we're in the heat of the moment. When our brain's fear center is activated, it overpowers our ability to think critically about what we're experiencing. We can only grow our emotional vocabulary and intelligence when we are calm.

However, we cannot achieve healing and emotional intelligence overnight. It took me multiple years, many trials, failures, conversations, and sessions with a therapist to unravel these root issues.

So what do we do in the meantime? How do we proceed when tensions are high, our heart is beating fast, and we feel like we're going to explode? We need tools to help us calm down right then to regain control.

As a child, around age eight, I would get absolutely furious. It was around the time my parents started having marital issues. I had a lot of emotions and zero coping skills. I would sob, I could scream—it was all extremes with me. My mom would squat down to my eye level, grab me tightly by the shoulders, and hold me there.

She would breathe slowly. In Mandarin, she would whisper, "Eric, I need you to count to ten. When you get this angry, I need you to count to ten. Okay? Can you do that for me?"

"Yi... er... san..." I would say through gritted teeth (meaning "One... two... three...").

I never understood the value of this tool she taught me until I got older. My inability to manage my own emotions was hurting my relationships.

The three best tools I've found for de-escalating in a moment of tension are:

1. Slow down: Don't say the first thing that comes to my mind. Wait at least twenty minutes before responding to the message. Stay in the car for a few extra minutes before going into the stressful situation.

2. Take a breath: Count to ten. When we're stressed, we stop breathing deeply, which only increases our inability to think clearly.

3. Leave the room to de-escalate: Go for a short walk and say what you're thinking out loud, but alone, like a practice run so you don't say something you'll regret. Go on a short run to give your body something else to focus on momentarily. Step away and journal what you're feeling. Call a friend who can act as a sounding board and help you see the situation objectively.

These steps aren't just for anger. These are also for when we're irritated, anxious, overwhelmed, overcome by sadness, or starting to withdraw. These tools help us calm down to communicate what we want to say at that moment rather than saying something we don't mean and picking up the pieces later.

Look, counting to ten will not change your life. But counting to ten will get you to the next moment. And in that moment, the seconds you take to breathe may give you slightly more clarity than you otherwise would have had. With even a bit more clarity, you can make a better decision—in that moment and the one after. And so on. The tools' impact is not drastic immediately, but it's like turning your steering wheel just a millimeter. The farther you travel, the more you will realize that while the change was small, you are far from where you would have been otherwise. That is what this book is all about.

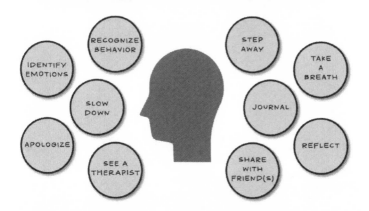

TOOLS FOR DEALING WITH EMOTIONS

RECOGNIZE BEHAVIOR · IDENTIFY EMOTIONS · SLOW DOWN · APOLOGIZE · SEE A THERAPIST · STEP AWAY · TAKE A BREATH · JOURNAL · SHARE WITH FRIEND(S) · REFLECT

➤ TOOLS FOR DEALING WITH EMOTIONS IN THE LONG-TERM

The growth I described in the conversation with Diana at the beginning of this chapter resulted from multiple factors. One was understanding more about traditional masculinity and where my hesitation around emotions came from, as we discussed two chapters ago. Another was building my emotional vocabulary, as discussed in the last chapter. Using these tools to have more authentic conversations with other men brought me enormous healing. And I also saw a therapist for a while where I processed how my childhood influences my relationships today.

I strongly recommend each of these steps. Ultimately, our emotions are a check engine light telling us something requires our attention. It's what we *do* with them that matters, and we are responsible for reclaiming our power over them. Do our actions move us closer or further away from our larger goals? Does the expression of our feelings build others up or tear them down? Your answer to these questions will determine whether you are winning or losing the fight for the person you want to become.

> Ultimately, our emotions are a check engine light telling us something requires our attention. It's what we *do* with them that matters, and we are responsible for reclaiming our power over them.

ACTION PLAN:
CLAIM YOUR EMOTIONS

In learning to regulate my emotions, I created the acronym A.C.T, representing: Acknowledge the emotion, Create space to process, and Talk through your feelings. I encourage you to practice this as a way of reclaiming your emotions. Take a moment and identify one semi-recent incident when you felt a strong emotion. Assuming it wasn't two minutes ago, you've likely had some distance from this event. Take this opportunity to investigate it and practice claiming your power over emotions and the experiences around you.

Step 1: Acknowledge the Emotion

1. Identify a moment when you felt a strong negative emotion
2. What emotion(s) did you feel? (See: Feelings Wheel in Chapter 7)
3. Take a moment to accept how you felt. It's okay that you felt that way.

Step 2: Create Space to Process

4. What happened to make you feel that way?
5. How did you react?
6. Is there another perspective from which you could see this situation?
7. Is there a better way of coping than you are right now?

Step 3: Talk Through Your Feelings

8. Who can you talk to about what you felt?
9. Is there anyone you need to apologize to?
10. Are there any boundaries or next steps you need to set?

STRATEGY THREE:

CREATE YOUR TEAM

CREATE YOUR TEAM

9

THE EPIDEMIC OF MALE ISOLATION

More and more these days, I meet men without anchors in relationships without roots.

—JON TYSON

As an athlete from a young age, I spent a lot of my time with other boys my age who played sports and the men who coached and trained us. Even though contact with my father waned as I entered adolescence, there was no lack of male influence in my life. It was a total surprise to me when I discovered a depth of connection with other men at twenty-eight that provided an essential element my life was missing.

Diana and I had been married for three years, and we relied primarily on each other. We were isolated socially and had become comfortable with that norm. We were, at least, until we found out that Diana was pregnant. We were overjoyed but also overwhelmed.

We both had messy family backgrounds but wanted to do this right and didn't know how. We knew we needed support and longed to feel part of a community. So although it was out of our norm, Diana and I accepted the invitation to join a group of families that met weekly in each other's homes. We dished our plates and entered the kitchen frenzy.

Within minutes, Diana was swept away by the other women, eager to ask about her pregnancy and share their own stories. I was led in the opposite direction and invited to sit with the men chatting, eating, and talking about basketball. I assumed their wives had pressured them into attending and the conversation was what I expected from a bunch of guys. *Nothing new here.*

However, as I kept coming back over the course of time, the conversations made a turn I wasn't expecting. They shifted from talking about food and basketball to what was going on in their lives. One man shared about a difficult challenge he didn't think he handled well at work that week. Another acknowledged he'd snapped at one of his kids and wondered if there was a better way he could have responded. One described a decision he and his wife were processing, and he was open to input from the group. For every story shared, the other men chimed in—sometimes with a serious tone, often with warm laughter. These groups became a safe space where we could talk about anything and everything.

Honestly, I was shocked. I had never been in a group of men where it felt like nothing was off-limits. I sensed that I had lived my whole life having conversations in the entryway without ever inviting anyone into the house. Marital struggles? I locked that door. Fears for the future? Locked. Insecurities and shortcomings? Locked. Dreams that may or may not come true? Locked. I'd never seen men talk about these things before. I never imagined it was possible until these relationships took root.

"What about you, Eric? How have you and Diana been doing?"

When one of the men asked me this question one night, I didn't *have* to be honest. I could have played into the belief that marital struggles were taboo to discuss, as my parents and others led me to believe as a child. Yet this environment felt so attractive to me that I lost all need to put on a false front. These were not just men I could have fun with but men who could make me a better version of myself.

I started off cautiously. "We've been good, excited for the baby." I talked about some of our concerns about the pregnancy. As they listened and asked questions, I realized with surprise that I felt safe. I decided to share more vulnerably. "Honestly, some things have been tough for me."

For the first time, I admitted to other men that I struggled with losing my temper. I was afraid that the rage that seemed to boil over from deep inside could undermine my ability to be a solid husband and a good parent.

While I was half-expecting the group to respond with judgment, shame, and that awkward silence, those negatives never came. The entire group listened to me and didn't give me simplistic "band-aid" answers. Some shared that they were working through similar things. Others encouraged me by recognizing that I owned the problem and wanted to grow. Many also shared their parenting experiences—mistakes they'd made and what they were doing about them.

I wasn't only surprised at how these men responded to me but how quickly I felt accepted by them. Granted, I was still getting to know them. But the safety I felt moved me past the fear of alienation. In response, they made talking this way seem normal. I saw that my issues were commonplace, which gave me hope that I could overcome the trials of this season. Their confidence in me gave me confidence in myself. Rather than feeling ashamed and misunderstood, I felt supported and empowered.

I realized what I'd been missing in my journey into manhood—other men who were on that same path who would travel with me. I had felt like I had no other men to turn to once my dad left us. For the first time since I was twelve, I realized that I no longer needed to go at it alone.

➤ THE MYTH OF THE SELF-MADE MAN

If asked why it seems so hard for men to grow into healthy adults, I'd say our trend of isolation is the first place to look. We're taught the false belief that a real man is self-made and succeeds by sheer grit and determination, never asking for help. Needing anyone else is a sign of weakness, and real men are strong and self-reliant.

If this is your idea of manhood, I have one question for you: How's that working for you?

Yeah, it didn't work for me, either.

Think about it this way: What would you do if you wanted to learn how to become a fantastic cook? Try to learn from cookbooks alone? You could, but it would be hard to master that insider knowledge that good cooks share. The best way to learn a skill is to get instruction from someone who knows how to do it. That's the reason why YouTube videos are so popular. If you want to learn how to build a cabinet or repair your washing machine, a video will show you how. We rely on others who have gone before us.

> I realized what I'd been missing in my journey into manhood—other men who were on that same path who would travel with me.

So how do you learn what it takes to deal with men's challenges? Connecting with other men is one sure way. The women in our lives can shape, challenge, and refine us, but they cannot show us how to be men. We need other men to mentor us and join us on the journey.

Just as a fighter never enters the ring alone, no man should face his fight alone. Rather, the people in our corner are often our greatest asset. Whether we're pushing through discomfort to heal our past, reconciling a relationship, creating better habits, living healthier, saving our marriages, or starting a business, we need others alongside us if we expect to win.

TRENDS IN MALE COMMUNITY

Most people feel lonely at some point in their lives. But for men especially, the research shows we've got work to do. In 1990, the Survey Center on American life collected data on American socializing. They compiled data again in 2021 to see how patterns had changed over those thirty years.

> ➤ Thirty years ago, 55% of men said they had at least six close friends. In 2021, that number dropped to an average of three close friends.
> ➤ Thirty years ago, 3% of men said they had no close friendships at all. In 2021, that number rose to 15% of men with no close friendships.
> ➤ Men with one to three close friends were almost as lonely as those without close friends. Data showed men needed to have several close friends to feel significantly less lonely.

These isolation trends were most severe for young people, especially young men.

> ➤ Thirty years ago, 45% of young men said they reach out to their friends first when facing a

personal problem. In 2021, that number dropped to 22%.

> In 2021, nearly one in five Americans reported having no close social connections. For men under thirty, one in four said they had no close social connections. [12]

As if loneliness isn't bad enough, social isolation is also a substantial health risk. Studies have shown that being isolated has health risks on par with smoking or lack of exercise. It's another reason why men need to face the fight for their connections. [13]

> OBSTACLES TO MALE CONNECTION

The problem lies in a simple fact—men tend to isolate and rely on themselves more often than to build relationships in which they can share openly and honestly. Most men I know struggle with loneliness. Yet when things get tough, and we need the most support, we tend to isolate ourselves.

> Just as a fighter never enters the ring alone, no man should face his fight alone. Rather, the people in our corner are often our greatest asset.

The perplexing question is why?

The most common reason for isolation is that "We're all so busy." While the pace of modern life certainly plays a role, I think there's much more to it. We often have the most friends in our early years; why is it so hard to bring those social ties with us and create new ones? What obstacles stand in the way?

For one, we lack the proximity we once had in school, college, or our hometown. In childhood, we tend to have friends we see often and talk to weekly, at least at school. In college, we also benefit from proximity, the opportunity for social events, and at the very least, set times we're forced to leave our cave and be with others. Perhaps all our friends have moved away, or the nearest friend is a thirty-minute commute. We try and plan something for two weeks from now, but it falls through.

On top of distance, work transitions can also inhibit connection. Sometimes your work schedules aligned, but then your friend's shift changes, and you can't find a time in common to meet. You might find yourself working more than one job, not having much free time left, let alone energy. Instead, you may benefit from an online connection. But what if you're relying on it as a guise of community when, in reality, you're not getting or giving the human connection you need?

The addition of romantic relationships can also make the connection with friends more difficult. When you or other friends enter a relationship or get married, the distribution of free time changes drastically. Now, a large chunk of your or their available time is eliminated, as nurturing a romantic relationship takes enormous work, and there is less relational energy to go around. When you add kids into the mix, the challenge increases exponentially. The new parent doesn't have much control over their time anymore, even as they still long for community.

When we enter new seasons of life, over time, we can struggle to connect over the things we once did. When our friends move into different seasons than us, we may not be able to relate to them anymore, and vice versa. We lose the "glue" to our relationships when the substance of our connection is based solely on proximity and shared experience. But a foundation in deeper shared values and longer-term life goals are more apt to stand the test of time.

As men, we rely more on proximity and shared experiences for our relational glue when we fail to build those deeper bonds. Men sometimes value doing activities together more than simply talking. While this can be a great starting point for connection, we depend on those activities for conversation. No one ever "breaks the ice" into a deeper bonding to create more solid relationships.

➤ THE TRUTH BEHIND OUR EXCUSES

Despite all these circumstantial explanations for our isolation, I believe our isolation comes down to our beliefs more than our circumstances. While we may feel that we're too busy, our connection is more a matter of how we prioritize it—or not. We often don't prioritize connections because we're buying into false beliefs we must identify and dismantle. What are those beliefs?

1. We buy into the lie that others wouldn't understand us when in reality, other men feel the same way we do. Therefore, they have a much greater capacity for empathy than we give them credit for, and so do we!
2. We buy into the lie that we become weaker by accepting support while having a team of people actually strengthens our weak points and blind spots.
3. We buy into the lie that we are a burden when we ask others for support, yet we allow others to live into their purpose when we let them support us.
4. We buy into the lie that relationships aren't as vital for us as they are for women. The reality is that we cannot simply rely on our partner as our only source of community. While the *way* we connect may look different, we cannot become the men we dream of being without that connection.

Do any of these resonate with you? What limits you from fully connecting with the other men in your life? What fears stand in the way?

The leap of faith I took to allow myself to be known deeply by other men opened my eyes to what I'd been missing. The payoff was immeasurable.

Since that day, I have aggressively sought out community in each area of my life. When I opened my gym, I sought out people who either had similar strengths and skills to me or who possessed strengths and skills I did not have so we could help one another grow. Those who helped me build my gym and those who first joined it were the initial men to validate this dream that I was in the process of externalizing. Their validation made it feel real, outside of myself. This community affirmed the value it brought to them, confirming for me that I was following my purpose. These are the people we need in our corner—those who help clarify our purpose and catalyze our power.

10

A WINNER'S MOST VALUABLE ASSET

A friend loves at all times, and a brother is born for a time of adversity.

—PROVERBS 17:17

I remember one Friday night, just after 9 p.m. I was sitting on the gym floor with some members, leaning up against the old white fridge that was still there from when I first set up in the building. I rested my head against the cold, white surface, listening to its low hum. It almost lulled me to sleep on the black floor mat, but a deep voice shook me alert again.

Brian was our oldest member, a Japanese man in his fifties. He was the first member who didn't find the gym through a personal connection—he just found us off the street and became part of the family. The rest of us at the gym always thought Brian looked very wise—maybe because he was three decades older than us. Still, something in his eyes and mannerisms always seemed to indicate that he'd been through a lot of life and still came out with great joy.

"What was that?" I twisted my body to face him, still slumped against the old fridge.

"I said how long have you been here today?" Brian asked.

"Since 5:30." I shook my head and chuckled weakly.

"You mean 5:30 *a.m.*?" He raised his thick, grey-streaked eyebrows.

I nodded.

"You're doin' that every day, aren't you?"

"Yep," I was smiling but the bags under my eyes gave away my waning zeal.

"How long has it been? Little over a year?"

"Almost two. Actually, our lease renewal is coming up in six months." I rubbed a hand over my face.

He paused and cocked his head at me. "You don't sound too happy about it."

I exhaled, turning to face him. "I'm just feeling worn out, man. I love doing this. This place is my dream, and it doesn't feel like work to me. But it's been almost two years, and honestly, I haven't even taken a paycheck for myself yet. Diana's been supporting us on her teacher's salary. I don't know how much longer I can stay open. I'm like, what if all this comes to nothing? What if I put my wife and me through all this, draining our entire savings, and it's just a pipe dream?"

The weight of worry for the gym all fell squarely on my shoulders. Even while living my dream, I felt an old sense of loneliness closing in on me all over again.

Brian was decades older than me, and I thought he might give me business advice on how to cut costs, raise profits, and hire other coaches to teach some classes.

Instead, he looked at me, put a hand on my shoulder, and said, "Eric, I don't know if this place will make it. But I know that *you* will."

That stopped me in my tracks.

My eyes brimmed with tears as those around us continued shouting, racking weights, and packing up for the day. I lowered my head and looked down at my crossed legs. I had no other older male figures or mentors at that point in my life. The way this older man spoke belief into me gave me this tangible sense of hope I didn't have before. While I was a fighter at heart, I'd been losing the fight to keep the gym open. His words put the fight back into me. It felt like I'd emotionally signed a new lease—a renewed commitment and determination to continue building this dream.

> "Eric, I don't know if this place will make it. But I know that *you* will."

I could have chosen not to share with Brian. We were at the gym, after all. We were helping build one another up physically, but that didn't necessarily mean he wanted to hear about my personal struggles. The gym was *my* baby, and I bore the weight of risk and sole responsibility for its future. I could have assumed my honest confession would be a burden. I could have guessed he wouldn't understand. He could have even judged me—a gym owner not believing in his own gym?! What an imposter. But no, that was the voice in my head, not his voice.

When I chose to be honest with him, right then and there I decided to let my guard down. Or maybe I was so tired my brain was not functioning coherently enough to put on a successful façade. Regardless, I made myself vulnerable to potential judgment, shaming, dismissal, and criticism. But even if those had occurred, my reward made the risk seem paltry. We made a shift from building one another up physically to reinforcing one another on a deeper level.

When it comes down to it, we cannot become the men we were meant to be alone. The rewards we gain from living in connection are too great to be outweighed by any risk, discomfort, or effort. Over the years, I have experienced countless benefits of living in connection, including but not limited to the following:

> - It inspires us to see possibilities beyond our own experiences.
> - It reveals the blind spots that are holding us back.
> - It shakes us out of our destructive thought patterns.
> - It provides external validation and support to the dreams within us.

> It keeps us accountable to the growth we want to see in ourselves.

> It gives us perspective by involving us in someone else's story outside of our own.

What Brian gave me that day propelled me forward in my fight in a way I could never have done for myself.

> DIVERSIFYING OUR CORNER

Another dynamic at play made this interaction even more meaningful: Brian was my friend, but he was also almost thirty years older than me. Every other member of the gym at that time was in their twenties. Had the encouragement come from them, it still would have been meaningful. However, the fact that it came from Brian uniquely impacted me. Because Brian was much older, his words carried an authority that a twenty-something's would not have. His words held the credibility of someone who had experienced more of the ups and downs of life. Perhaps his own disappointments, false starts, failures, and triumphs, compiled over the years gave him a uniquely elevated perspective on what I was going through. When he encouraged me, he did so with not just the kindness of a friend but with the authority of a father figure. He saw a better vision for me in a moment when all I saw was a dead end.

> When it comes down to it, we cannot become the men we were meant to be alone.

This moment shows us that we need a variety of connections to nurture us into the men we're supposed to be. We lose something valuable if our peers are the only people in our corner. Yet if all our friends were twenty years older, we'd also miss out on the value of growing with someone in our life stage. And because Brian chose to spend time with a bunch of twenty-somethings, he was able to live into his purpose and catalyze younger men to do the same.

To achieve a rich, varied web of connections, we need these types of people present:

1. Role Models: People "out there" who we can look up to and gain inspiration from, even if we don't know them personally.
2. Mentors: People who are older than us or more experienced than us in a particular area. As opposed to role models, we know our mentors personally, and they are paying attention to us, seeing and nurturing our growth.
3. Peers: People who can be our *resonators*, validating and authentically understanding what we're going through. When we're in the same experience or life stage, peers offer us a different lens to see the same situation, and we are fulfilled by doing the same for them.
4. Mentees: People younger than us or less experienced in a particular area. They remind us that our purpose is about more than ourselves, and

they give us the privilege of being part of their journey toward purpose.

When you look at your corner, do you have people like this present? As we face our fight, these people provide us with a model our family may not have given us. These people inspire, encourage, and give us a fresh perspective. We train alongside them, and they hold us accountable to our goals. They believe in us when we fail to believe in ourselves. Their words have the power to put fresh fuel in our tank. Our corner is our most valuable asset.

11

HOW TO ASSEMBLE
YOUR CORNER

*You're the average of the five people
you spend the most time with.*

—JIM ROHN

I recently brought my five-year-old daughter Harper to work with me for the day. Bundled in a gray Minnie Mouse sweater, she sat opposite my desk with her iPad and some Goldfish. She followed me around the gym, chatting with members and playing with gym equipment as I took care of my tasks.

We'd been having some good conversation as she asked questions about what I was doing, and I explained it to her. Suddenly, she looked up and told me, "One of my friends always calls me stupid."

My first instinct was to ask, "Where does this kid live?" But as I took a deep breath, another thought struck me. *If this kid calls my daughter stupid, I wonder what she gets called at home.* Regaining my adult composure, I realized this was not an opportunity to beat up a five-year-old. It was an opportunity to teach my daughter how to choose her friends.

I knelt down to Harper's level. "Do you know what stupid means?"

"It means not smart," she said.

"Is that true about you?"

She thought about it for a second. "No, it's not true."

"That's right, Harper. So did she tell you the truth, or was it a lie?"

She thought again. "It was a lie."

"That's right. Harper, if you have friends who aren't telling you the truth, do you want to spend time with those people? Why choose to be with someone who tells you lies? We should spend time with people who use their words to build us up, not tear us down."

She nodded at me and then resumed hopping across barbell plates as if they were lily pads. Just like that, she had moved on, but I continued to revel in the power of that conversation. This was one of the most spontaneous yet meaningful conversations I've had with my five-year-old, and this is a lesson many adults haven't figured out.

➤ AUDITING OUR SPHERES OF INFLUENCE

Who we spend our time with is who we become. "Show me your five closest friends, and I'll show you your next five years." I can't count how many times I've said that.

The truth is this: the people we surround ourselves with either tell us the truth or lie. Sometimes we don't know their lies are lies. So these people plant beliefs in our hearts about who we are. As time goes on, we internalize the things we were told at five years of age, and we become an eleven-, twenty-five-, or forty-year-old saying, "I can't do that because I'm stupid."

The people we choose to spend time with shape our perception of reality. We need to monitor who's influencing us as frequently as we'd monitor our finances. It's like auditing our credit card statements and finding out: *Oh no! I've been paying for Hulu monthly, but I haven't used it in a year!* Even while you forgot about it, it continued to draw money from your account. The same goes for the people in our lives. Our attention is our currency. Sometimes we are still paying people our attention when we should have stopped a long time ago.

Is there anyone whose influence in our lives should have been canceled a long time ago, but we didn't see it? Are there people in our circle who are telling us lies about ourselves? Are there people we spend time with who aren't making us better versions of ourselves? We should be looking for people with the following qualities:

> ‣ They use their words to build us up rather than tear us down.
> ‣ They are actively working toward growth in their own lives.

- They pursue healthy relationships with those around them.
- They press outside of their comfort zones.
- They're honest about real issues and encourage us to be honest too.
- They're not afraid to hold us accountable or be held accountable for our goals.

> INFLUENCE BOUNDARIES

Sometimes we outgrow people, especially when we begin orienting our lives in a new direction. Recently, one of my coaches told me about a friend of his who was trying to pull him back into some destructive old habits my coach had already outgrown. When I asked my coach why he was still friends with this guy, he shrugged and said, "History." Often, we continue letting someone influence us not because we value their influence or they make us better but because they have been around for so long. Don't get me wrong—there is value and a sense of groundedness in having friends you've known forever. However, it can be damaging when their influence in your life is incongruous with your goals—when they are not helping you win your fight but diverting your attention from it.

> Sometimes we outgrow people, especially when we begin orienting our lives in a new direction.

What if the person or people holding you back from winning are part of your family? Maybe a parent still wants you to pursue a career you know you're not supposed to have. It could be a sibling who instigates arguments and digs up old wounds. Maybe it's a spouse who continues buying unhealthy food when you've expressed wanting to eat healthier. Scenarios like this can feel a bit more complex.

However, whether it's with friends, family, or anyone else, auditing our circle doesn't necessarily mean cutting people off. If someone intentionally uses their words to tear you down, perhaps the relationship should be ended. However, in many cases, that friend you have so much history with doesn't need to be dead to you just because they're not moving you toward your life goals. Similarly, you don't have to cut off all your family ties to keep your diet. We can value someone's influence in our lives in one area, even if we reject it in another. We can keep the good parts of the relationship while filtering out the bad influence.

Auditing your circle means intentionally placing "influence boundaries." That means we can choose which ways we allow someone to influence us rather than accepting their influence entirely. For example, someone may be terrific at finance, but not the best spouse. You want their influence over your budgeting, but you don't need to take marriage advice from them. Perhaps you avoid that topic of conversation. If you can't, you can still consciously reflect on the fact that their marriage values do not align with yours. Articulate what yours are early on.

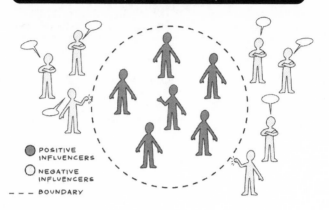

POSITIVE INFLUENCERS
NEGATIVE INFLUENCERS
- - - BOUNDARY

Similarly, if you have a friend with lots of history, allow them to influence your reminiscing as you reflect on the power of your shared past. But if you gave up drinking and they're still getting drunk every weekend, you might set a boundary that you don't go out with them when they do. Maybe you choose to spend less time with them and invest more of that time into other friendships.

In your family, you can still spend time with them but communicate that certain topics of conversation are off-limits and remove yourself when they come up. If your spouse isn't taking your nutrition goals seriously, perhaps you can arrange to do the grocery shopping and agree on a few places where you both like to eat. Tell them when you plan to exercise this week and help arrange for childcare if you need to protect that time. All in all, we can remain in a relationship with people while taking greater intentionality to control how their mindsets and habits shape our own.

⟩ YOUR PERSONAL BOARD OF DIRECTORS

I learned over time that I needed to assemble a team of people to help me live up to my highest potential—like how a CEO has a Board of Directors. To that end, I created a "board of directors" for my life. This group consists of men I most respect and admire—those who know me and my vision for my life, as well as their own. I give this group unfettered access to my life. Full transparency. My bank statements, arguments with my wife, my worst parenting moments, my biggest wins, my deepest dreams, and my core values. Nothing is off-limits.

Each person on my board of directors brings something different to the table based on the strengths I admire in their lives. There are some I ask more about financial decisions, and others I ask about marital growth, parenting, or faith. For example, I ask my wife and two other people before any important financial decision. A hundred people could say one thing, but these three people's input would carry more gravity.

While my board of directors and other closest friends all have different strengths and perspectives, they also have core traits in common. These traits align with our deepest values and growth areas this season, so we can spur one another on. My closest circle works out, cares about what they eat, lives beneath their means rather than overspending, and they work toward great relationships, healthy marriages, and healthy relationships with their children. Lastly, they have a big-picture vision for their lives and actively pursue big goals. These are not topics we quietly harbor as we talk about surface-level things. We discuss these things regularly, checking in, encouraging, and challenging one another in our goals.

I encourage the young men I coach to consider who would be on their board of directors. We tend to think only "really important people" need a board of directors. To that I say: *you are important.* Your success is just as critical as the success of any person or business out there. Why not treat yourself that way?

Inevitably, who we spend time with shapes who we become. But who in your life would you want to shape who you become? Whose life do you admire, not just for what they have, but for their character, the choices they've made, and the wins they've intentionally invested into over time?

> Your success is just as critical as the success of any person or business out there. Why not treat yourself that way?

If you want more of these people in your life, what communities can you invest more into to meet people and go deeper? Whether this is at work, at the locations you frequent, through a hobby you enjoy, or through a church you attend, what communities can you join to receive and offer connection?

Ultimately, the people we spend time with are the ones who shape who we become. We have the opportunity to prioritize connection against the trend of male loneliness.

ACTION STEP:
BUILD YOUR BOARD OF DIRECTORS

1. Who are your closest friends? Write their names.
2. Out of your close friends and others, who would you want on your board of directors? Note: this doesn't necessarily mean who you spend the most time with; it's more about who you feel you can be honest with, who's honest with you, who inspires you to become better, and whose life you admire.
3. What strengths does each person on that list have, as evidenced by their life? List them under each name.
4. Tell each of these people what you admire about their lives and that you want them to help shape you. Ask what their goals are in life and how you can support them.
5. Is there anyone whose influence on your life you'd like to limit? In what ways can you limit their influence?

STRATEGY FOUR:

CHALLENGE YOUR STORY

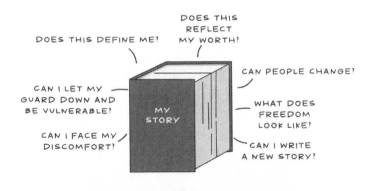

DOES THIS DEFINE ME?

DOES THIS REFLECT MY WORTH?

CAN PEOPLE CHANGE?

CAN I LET MY GUARD DOWN AND BE VULNERABLE?

MY STORY

WHAT DOES FREEDOM LOOK LIKE?

CAN I FACE MY DISCOMFORT?

CAN I WRITE A NEW STORY?

CHALLENGE YOUR STORY

12

THE BATTLE BETWEEN DOING AND BEING

We are human beings, not human doings.
—UNKNOWN

I practically floated off the stage and down the steps, still soaking in the crowd's roar of claps and cheers from the event I had just won. I finished faster than everyone by what felt like minutes, although it was only seconds.

Throwing a towel over my neck, I wiped my sweat and walked through the aisle of bright tents. My body filled with a euphoric high—the adrenaline rush that accompanies lifting onstage and calling every muscle in your body into action. I let my heart rate slow down as the cool breeze tingled against my face. As I approached our gym EZ Up tent, I saw my wife, Diana, and friends cheering, and I couldn't help but smile.

"Hey, saved a seat for our winner! Want something to eat before the next event?"

My friend pulled out the camping chair, and I lowered myself to sit down. However, the second I bent to sit, a ripple of sharp pain shot through the left side of my lower back. I lost control of the muscle for a few moments as it spasmed. It was agonizing, like claws sinking into the muscle. The pain was debilitating.

"Woah, you okay? What just happened?" my friends jumped to my side.

"I think I'm okay. I got this sharp pain in my back. I think I just had a muscle spasm."

I had never experienced something like that before and fear immediately consumed me. I had heard stories like this before about an injury that ended someone's weightlifting career.

After a few minutes, the pain died down to a bearable ache.

"It's feeling a bit better now. I think after the next event, I'll get it checked—"

"The next event? No, there's no way you're going to go out there again today." Diana shot me a look.

My heart sank. I was set on finishing, but Diana talked me out of it. It was a recreational event, there was nothing on the line, and I had nothing to lose by leaving except for my pride.

I knew it could be a substantial injury, but I remained in denial about the possible severity. I did rest it for three or four days, and it still hurt, but I wouldn't wait. I popped some Advil and went back to my regular training routine as if nothing had happened.

"Hey, you're back already? You need to take some time off," my friend said. I continued to load up the weight on my bar.

"Gotta keep training. We've got the next competition in a month!"

He frowned at me, turning to face me more seriously. "You need to let that back heal, man, or it will get way worse. If you hurt it again while it's still healing, you may mess it up for life. It's not worth it!"

I sighed, put the weights back on the rack, walked around the room a little, and went home.

Over the following weeks, I tried to take it easy. I would train when I could, then think about training when I couldn't. But eventually, I stopped training competitively altogether. Days turned into weeks, then months. While the physical discomfort was terrible, the mental distress was far worse. The longer I stayed away from training the way I used to, the darker my mental state became. I began feeling aimless and depressed.

The fear gnawing at my mind was this: what if I can never compete again? What if I'm no longer a competitor? Something about this ached worse than my back. I thought of myself as an athlete, a contender. I was pursuing this goal of competing at a higher level. All my actions were tied to this. I planned out my schedule, meals, habits, and life around this identity. Now I felt like it was all going up in flames.

➤ WHAT STORY ARE YOU TELLING YOURSELF?

Transition, change, and crisis are all characterized by extreme discomfort. While no one likes to feel this way, this agitation offers us a unique window into ourselves. These moments are rich in opportunity for self-discovery!

While I didn't enjoy this season, it revealed a valuable discovery about myself: beneath my identity as an athlete and competitor, I didn't know who I was. That's why I was willing to go to great lengths to continue competing, even risking my long-term health and mobility for the short-term payoff. I had pinned my whole sense of self on what I could do and accomplish rather than on who I wanted to be.

I could have just tried to recover quickly and get back on the path I was on. However, this revelation was disturbing to me. Have you ever had that experience? When something important was ripped away from you, for whatever reason, and it alarmed you to realize how empty you felt when it was gone? I longed to have a more profound sense of self outside of competitions. I didn't want that one part of my life to be all I was. After all, what would I do when I got older and couldn't compete anymore? If I kept running, it would catch up with me sooner or later. I knew I needed

> I had pinned my whole sense of self on what I could do and accomplish rather than on who I wanted to be.

to understand what I felt right then to get to the root of my discomfort.

As I dug deeper, I began to see a cause and theme I hadn't wanted to admit. So many layers covered the truth that it had remained neatly hidden. But now, as I reached the depths of why not competing felt so uncomfortable, I could see it was because it made me feel important. Special. Significant. Valuable. When I felt insecure, remembering my identity and accomplishments in this area made me feel better about myself. While this worked in the short run, it couldn't help me in the long term because the absence of this band-aid showed me I had a deeper wound that had never healed.

This fear that I wasn't valuable had roots far deeper than this moment. As I worked through this depression in therapy and with my wife and friends, it became apparent that it tied back to a story I developed about myself in childhood. The story originated when my dad left, even before the day of the gunshots. I knew my dad did not leave because of me; many other factors were at play. But I could not understand this back then. I think any child whose parent has left them grows up wondering whether it was their fault—wondering how they could have been better, more, enough. They ponder why they were insufficient to prevent the relationship from falling apart. Many boys who grow up as children of divorce build strong but false exteriors to hide their hidden insecurities. I was one of them. And there I was, still one—even years later, as a grown man.

Beneath my external accomplishments, there was still a little boy inside me asking, "Am I good enough? Or do I need to win another medal? How can I prove myself? What can I do to show you?" Growing up, I craved this validation in my friendships and sports, especially basketball. Then, I craved it from those I associated with as a higher-level CrossFit athlete. That was simply the next cycle of an old story that kept repeating itself because I hadn't yet challenged it.

The CrossFit culture uniquely met my need for validation. CrossFit athletes had this reputation for not just being fit but for being the fittest of the fit. These athletes did not just perform simple workout movements; they made their athleticism into a show. I gravitated toward this as it filled this need in me for validation—it assured me I was skilled, important, valuable, and praised. It filled a hole in me—a void where a healthier sense of identity should have been.

> I wanted to challenge my story by no longer hinging my sense of self purely on what I could *do* and then figuring out who I truly *was*.

But other than the praise of others for my physical performance, I had nothing. So when I was injured and could no longer be the best of the best, I returned to being nothing.

It was extremely uncomfortable to admit this to myself. In many ways, facing this pattern in my life made me feel like a scared little boy again rather than the strong man I'd worked to become. However, I needed to confront this habit in all its facets, or I'd risk this same derailing every time I got an injury, lost a competition, or experienced a setback. That was not how I wanted to live. I wanted to challenge my story by no longer hinging my sense of self purely on what I could *do* and then figure out who I truly *was*.

➤ THE BATTLE BETWEEN DOING AND BEING

The shift I began undertaking took me from doing to being. You may already be familiar with this dichotomy, or you may not be. Either way, it's a monumental concept where you press into discomfort to explore who you are at your core. It's especially effective during the transitions of young adulthood. I find it's also helpful to revisit and articulate afresh as our life seasons and sources of identity shift over time.

In essence, our identity is in a state of constant tension between doing and being. Our sense of identity can often become disproportionately focused on what we do over who we are.

"Doing" means the actions we take, roles we occupy, accomplishments we claim, and the habits we engrave. Sometimes, doing is backed by intentional thought; often, it's automatic. What we do is an expression of our goals or ideologies. Our minds constantly monitor and evaluate our current situation against a model or standard in our heads—against some idea of what we desire, require, expect, or fear. When we find a discrepancy between how things are and how we think they should be, we act on it—whether it's getting a snack, joining a competition, or saying we're sorry.

While what we do feeds into who we are, and vice versa, focusing too much on what we do can become a trap. When we think of what we do as the substance of who we are, we define ourselves by an action. We become trapped in a cycle of obligation. We tell ourselves we need to continue that action, say yes, stay in the relationship, or keep the hated job to be okay. Anytime we think "I have to," "I must," or "I should," we are focusing our identity on doing. We *do* to reinforce who we *are*, but after a while, the two become disconnected. Our actions no longer lead us toward our identity but away from it. And we are constantly striving to upkeep something that is long gone.

SO, WHAT DO YOU DO?

In America, especially, there is an excessive emphasis on defining ourselves by what we produce. What's the first thing we ask when we meet someone? "So, what do you do?" While it can be a great starting point for conversation, it can sometimes make us feel like our job is the most important thing about us. Research illustrates that most of us have internalized this belief. A 2014 Gallup study says that in the US, 55% of the employed say they get their sense of identity from their job, rather than it being "just what they do for a living." For those who graduated college, that number rises even higher, to 70%.[14]

While it's fulfilling to enjoy our work, our circumstances and security are often outside our control. According to the American Psychological Association, "Research on unemployment shows that losing one's job is detrimental to mental health—and often physical health—even without serious financial strain."[15] I know that sinking feeling from my personal experience and those I've coached. When our work falls through, we don't just wonder how we will provide, but we begin to wonder who we are.

"Being" is acknowledging our sense of self outside of our actions, roles, accomplishments, or habits. What does our internal landscape look like when we sit still? Being represents our character, values, and uniqueness. When prioritizing our being, we no longer depend on external circumstances for our happiness, assurance, and satisfaction.

Let's look at some examples that differentiate our doing from our being.

"Doing" identity: We tie this to circumstances and roles in different life seasons. Our *doing* identity very much shapes who we become and partially defines us for a season. However, it is not the entire substance of who we are because it may not always be present and may change over time.

Example:

I run a gym
I coach my clients
I drop off my kids at school
I am writing a book
I go to church
I live in California
I participate in mentorship groups
I host a podcast

"Being" identity: It remains consistent throughout life's seasons and grows in meaning and complexity as we grow to understand it. The defining feature of our *being* identity is that it is not dependent on our circumstances or roles, so it can't be lost to factors outside our control.

Example:

I am a learner
I am grateful
I am worthy
I am loved
I am resilient
I am a person of integrity
I am welcoming
I am invested in others

Our being identity is something we discover with greater clarity over time. To clarify, we have natural talents, skills, passions, and interests waiting for us to uncover them. There are innate, unique pieces of ourselves we cannot fake. Maybe we think, "Doesn't everyone feel that way? Doesn't everyone like doing that?" But no, not everyone does. There are traits uniquely designed within you.

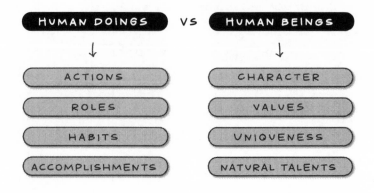

This discovery is not something we do passively; discovering our identity requires action! Remember your mom saying, "You don't know if you like it until you try it," as she shoved new foods onto your plate? Well, she was right. We don't know what we like until we try it. Likewise, we don't know if we're good at something until we attempt it! The choices we make and how we feel about them afterward will help us evaluate and identify our strengths and passions. The more we experience in this way, the more we discover ourselves.

As we discover key parts of our identity, we can choose to neglect or nurture them. If nurtured, our identity will evolve in meaning and complexity. However, it will remain consistent throughout our seasons and roles. These pieces of our identity can ground our sense of self when circumstances and people change our lives.

WAYS TO PRACTICE JUST BEING

1. Create space to be by yourself.
2. Choose a book just because it interests you; guilty pleasures are allowed.
3. Invest in a hobby, read a book, watch a video, or take a class. If you don't have a hobby, try one.
4. Take an opportunity to travel. Is there a trip you've been meaning to go on? On a smaller scale, can you take an overnight trip to a place you've wanted to see? Or even just try out a new restaurant, hiking trail, or coffee shop in an area you rarely frequent.

While the season of healing after my injury was bleak at times, the forced space away from competition healed something profound in how I saw myself. With a bit of distance from the world of competition, I could see it from a new perspective. After a while, I realized that not competing wasn't the worst thing that could happen to me. Diana supported me. My friends from the gym still reached out to check on me rather than forgetting I existed. I actually felt rested after a while, as my schedule was no longer jam-packed.

I still loved to exercise, but I needed it to serve me in a different way than it had before. While I previously used it to fight the feeling of being worthless, I began to use it to affirm the worth I already had. I took things slower, more carefully, and I was more intentional about my movements. I gave my body the respect it deserved. It was not worth sacrificing my long-term health to win this guise of being the best—until the next person who could lift a little more than me came along. I could genuinely cheer on others when I wasn't so busy comparing myself to them. I felt more grateful, supportive of others, and connected to the people around me. While I had defined myself as a competitor, ironically, I felt more likely myself than I had in a long time.

Rather than my actions determining who I was, it was who I was that began to determine my actions. Instead of being controlled by my fitness goals, I began tailoring my fitness to meet my life goals. I still wanted to be an athlete, but I also wanted to be strong in my mindset, connections, and rest.

Over time, as I began to articulate the difference between what I did and who I was, one of my coaches settled on this list to describe who I am:

> - I am a follower: I am a student and learner in every situation I encounter. I'm committed to growing, being committed, teachable, driven, and loyal.
> - I am a leader: I am centered, honest, and focused on my mission. I am caring and observant so I can teach and nurture others' gifts.
> - I am an athlete: I am humble, passionate, and driven in my pursuit of health. I am focused on my goals and the goals of others.

> ▸ I am a lover: I am expressive, not silent, with my affection. I am dedicated to my relationships, and I will give to others with joy and generosity.

These traits are not seasonal or tied to a role or position. They connect to the core of who I am, what I value, and my purpose in all contexts.

Most people never explore their identity or articulate the raw core of who they are. But when we do so, we take ownership of the story we believe about ourselves. We know that our identity is not dependent on our followers, titles, or trophies. It is also not dependent on the expectations of others or the old, disempowering stories we learned at some point. As we live a life that reflects this, we claim victory in our fight.

13

THE GIFT OF NEW OPPORTUNITIES

Without the rain, there is no beauty in summer.
Rain gives depth, it gives beauty, and it gives roots.
If a plant is only exposed to the sun and no rain, it
becomes dry, flimsy, and dead. Too many times we
curse the rain in our lives—suffering, trials, hardships—
but the truth is, without rain, nothing grows.

—JEFFERSON BETHKE

I sat in my gym office, scrolling through eBay listings for trucks in my area. None of them were very impressive, but every single one was better than the truck I had. In the dim room, my phone lit up beside me.

What does he want? I sighed, as I slowly picked up the phone.

"Hey." I continued scrolling.

"What are you doing?" my dad asked.

"Looking at trucks online. I'm thinking about leasing one for my gym."

"Mmm." He'd seen my truck. I could picture him nodding in agreement through the phone.

"I'll probably go to the dealership this weekend."

A pause.

"I want to go look at some cars too. I'll go with you."

"Oh." I moved my hand away from the mouse. "Okay, sure. I'll meet you there. How's nine?"

I couldn't remember the last time we spent time together. I felt nervous and I kept my expectations low in case things went south. I half expected he wouldn't show up at all.

But there he was, at nine o'clock sharp, standing in front of the building beneath a big red banner announcing their sales, with his hand held out against the sun. As I parked and walked up to him, we nodded at each other and started pacing down a line of Chevys. We strolled the lot for about an hour, talking about the trucks. I liked some trucks, but I wasn't quite ready to make the purchase. He didn't seem to find what he was looking for either. We parted and went home. Fairly uneventful.

One week later, he called me again.

"Hey, I bought you a truck." He said it as casually as if he'd bought me a sandwich. And I'd have been surprised by the sandwich.

"*You did what?*" I shook my head from side to side in disbelief. "No, no, no, it's okay. Thank you, but no."

"It's yours," he said matter-of-factly. "It's waiting for you at the dealership." He hung up.

. I had no choice but to pick it up from the dealership. My body was tense the whole drive home. There was room in the driveway, but I parked on the street in front of my house. It felt alien, like it didn't belong to me. Just looking at it made me feel anxious. Why would he give me this extravagant gift? I kept waiting for the other shoe to drop. I couldn't remember a time he'd given me something with no strings attached. I didn't understand what he wanted and didn't want to owe him anything.

Confused and suspicious, I left it on the street for four months without touching it. The one or two times I drove it, I treated it like it was someone else's car. If I drove it, I cleared all my stuff out of it once I was parked, making sure there was no trace I'd even been there. Every day, I drove my old '98 Tacoma, ready to return the truck at any second.

› THE OPPORTUNITY TO LIVE A NEW STORY

One day, I needed to move a piece of equipment for the gym, and I knew there wasn't enough space in my truck. I considered renting a U-Haul, trying to ignore the obvious solution sitting in front of my house. Finally, I walked out and looked at the spacious bed of the sparkling new Chevy. I sighed. That bed was why I needed it. *Okay, I will use it for this one thing, and then it's going right back in its spot.* I slid into it cautiously and gently turned the key. Inside, the faux leather still smelled brand new, and the plastic covered the LCD screen. I intended to keep it that way.

I parked farther away at the gym so no one would notice it. But as I walked in, one of my members stopped me—a guy in his fifties with two kids in high school.

He slapped me on the back. "Hey Eric, did you get a new truck?"

I hesitated. I wasn't eager to explain. "Yeah… I mean, kind of. I barely ever drive it."

He raised his eyebrows with concern.

"Is there something wrong with it?"

I struggled to explain the complicated relationship with my dad. "I'm grateful he bought it for me but driving it feels weird. I mean, I didn't earn it. It was just *given* to me."

The man rubbed his short beard, nodding for a moment. When he looked back at me, he said, "It's a beautiful thing that your dad bought you that truck. That's *your* truck. It was a gift. You didn't need to earn it—that's kind of the point." He chuckled. "I think your dad would love it if you drove it."

His words struck me. Of course it was my truck. Of course my dad wanted me to drive it. Why did I have such a hard time receiving it? Have you ever received a gift you couldn't bring yourself to accept?

I thought back on my life. Until then, my dad had never given me anything with no strings attached. When I was entering college, he offered to help pay for my tuition.

His father and family placed an extremely high value on education, and he felt that if I got a good education, I'd have a good life. However, that gift came with conditions. He'd pay for my tuition *if* I kept my grades to a certain standard and reported them to him every semester. It felt like his "gift" just gave him another power source to hold over me and control my life.

I was now asking myself, "Is he trying to buy me? Is he trying to erase history? Buy me a truck and call it all even?" I kept looking for the catch. I had a valid reason to hesitate and see if his gift was genuine, but he hadn't asked me for a thing in four months.

As I dug into the discomfort of this feeling, it revealed an old story I still believed. I believed that giving was an assertion of power rather than an act of love and that nothing was truly free. It was ridiculous because I loved giving to others and didn't give for a power play. But I never wanted to be on the *receiving* end! That fact alone revealed the power dynamic I still held in my mind. I felt comfortable as the giver because I was in power—no one could hold anything over me. As a receiver, I felt vulnerable; I risked being let down or manipulated. His giving me the truck was an act of love, and I wasn't willing to believe that he loved me. I resisted driving the truck as a way of keeping my guard up, afraid that if I let it down, things wouldn't work out.

Beyond fearing things wouldn't work out, I also feared things *would* work out. It seems nonsensical. I mean, why would I be afraid of having a good relationship with my dad? But when all you've ever known is disappointment, it becomes the norm. The norm is comfortable. Imagine the most challenging relationship in your life suddenly experiencing a change, and everything is different. You finally quit that job you've hated for so long. You start that business you've dreamed of for years. You break out of that addiction or that unhealthy relationship. You and your brother are finally on good terms. Of course, you want it—at least in theory. But what comes next? How does that freedom look? It's new and unknown, which is still terrifying. Both failure and success carry discomfort we must face.

While my wariness was valid, there remained a dissonance between my actions and values. I claimed to value forgiveness. I said I believed people could change and shattered relationships could be mended over time. I declared to want the unbroken families that other people had. But my actions screamed that I hadn't forgiven my dad, he and our relationship couldn't change, and I didn't want reconciliation enough to risk disappointment again. His mistakes were weighty. But decades later, he broke a pattern in our relationship by giving me a free gift. Was I willing to break the pattern by accepting it?

> Both failure and success carry discomfort we must face.

In moments like that, we must understand something important: what we do doesn't make who we are. Yet what we do reinforces or contradicts who we become. After all, we can't call ourselves a basketball player if we don't play basketball. We can't call ourselves a writer unless we write. We can't call ourselves forgiving unless we forgive. In that moment, my actions contradicted who I claimed to be. I was losing my fight because I was running from the discomfort of the risk at hand.

I needed to face my discomfort to realize I was denying myself the opportunity I'd longed for my entire life. My dad wasn't trying to erase history; he was trying to take a step in the right direction. He wasn't attempting to control me; he was helping me. He had probably been trying to love me in the best way he knew how for a long time, and I didn't have the eyes to see his effort through his mistakes. I was fighting him, but the real opponent was within me.

I realized if I wanted to win this fight, I needed to know when to let my guard down. After that conversation at the gym, I slowly started driving the truck more often. Each time I did it, the "what if"s came to my mind. As I persevered through these thoughts, I trained my mind, repeatedly responding to those fears and doubts. I taught my mind to trust— to trust my dad, trust that people can change, and most of all, trust my resilience to handle whatever

> What we do doesn't make who we are. Yet what we do reinforces or contradicts who we become.

would happen as a grown man and not a little boy. Each time I repeated this rhythm in my brain, I slowly accepted that I could receive his gift.

It turns out, it was worth the risk. Years later, he has never held his gift over me. I have, however, expanded my capacity for the discomfort of receiving. I have practiced vulnerability with people who want to help, so I can both give and receive generously, without fear. I had to challenge the old story that receiving made me unsafe and that needing help made me weak. In its place, I have trained my brain in the new story that receiving is a way of accepting love as I give it. And if the other person does choose to take advantage of me, I am strong enough to recover from that, it does not reflect my worth, and it is worth the risk. My new story has come a long way from the old one. It is evidence that I am winning my fight.

Whatever it looks like, we all have moments when our actions align more with our old story than our new one. It is an opportunity for us. And while we may not want or know how to accept it, it is a gift to us that ushers us into a new story, starting with these critical moments. I encourage you to identify these areas of dissonance in your own life—in your relationships, habits, and thought patterns. Where do your actions need to catch up to who you are? Where in your life is your new story waiting to be written?

14

NEW HABITS BIRTH A NEW STORY

Every action you take is a vote for the type of person you wish to become.

—JAMES CLEAR, ATOMIC HABITS

In the last year, my family of four became a family of five as our new baby Bailey joined the clan. Now with three young kids, Diana decided to take time off from being a teacher. I supported this. But as we grew closer and closer to the due date, I began feeling increasingly anxious about our financial situation. We weren't struggling to pay the bills exactly, but our list of expenses multiplied. It started to dominate most of my attention and thoughts throughout the day. This was a fear I often felt—an increasing internal pressure that I needed to support a family of five on my single income.

When I needed to make financial decisions, the driving force behind them became fear of not having enough. I remember constantly watching my parents argue and worry over money when I was a child. And when I made the leap of faith to open my gym instead of pursuing a more traditionally secure career path, I thought I'd overcome this fear. My decision paid off significantly because it aligned with my purpose rather than others' expectations of me. But now, that once-conquered belief began popping up again, saying, "No matter how much you earn, you won't have enough."

It was another old story trying to lull me into a fearful yet comfortable cycle. It gave me a sense of comfort to obsess over our bills and budget because it gave me a false sense of progress and control. *We won't be able to go broke as long as I continuously worry about it.* That was a lie. Yes, our finances needed attention and shifting to account for our growing family. But that was a practical matter, and Diana and I could deal with it. Consuming myself with worry and fear was not necessary for us to be okay.

Not only was this a lie, but it also contradicted what I claimed to believe about myself. I thought of myself as a grateful person and a generous person. Gratitude and generosity were two of my highest values. Yet the more I worried over our finances, the more distant I became from both. They represented the man I was supposed to be, but neither represented how I behaved during that time. Because the more I worried, the more I focused on what we didn't have. The deficits—or potential deficits—loomed largely, and what we already had appeared more meager. Not only that, but I became afraid to give generously, missing opportunities to help or bless others. The dissonance grew.

At some point, I was talking with my mentor, Chris Cooper. I felt so worried and discouraged and ultimately stuck in that cycle. I told him I wanted to be more grateful and more generous. "But how do I become grateful when I don't *feel* very grateful right now? I don't want to pretend to be grateful!"

He said something that shook me awake. "Gratitude is a practice." He explained that gratitude is not something we need to fake or manufacture, but it's also not something we must wait for our circumstances to provide for us.

I put my palm to my face; this mirrored something I had told my coaching clients repeatedly throughout my career! We may never act if we wait for our feelings to precede our actions. Sometimes, our actions must lead, and our emotions must follow. No, we cannot simply manufacture a sense of gratitude out of thin air. However, gratitude is not merely a feeling. It is an action. That means we can practice it even when we don't feel it.

I finally realized I needed to face my fight again and confront the discomfort of trusting that we would have enough. I needed these traits to be true of me, despite my circumstances, to live into the new story I wanted. Mastery of gratitude would require practice. I just needed to figure out how I would do it.

I had an idea and talked it out with my coaching staff. We started a new tradition at our gym, "Bright Spot Fridays." During cooldowns, people share their bright spot of the week—reached a fitness goal, got a raise at work, their mom is in remission, got to see a friend. It would start slowly, but as more people shared, it would help others recall the bright spots in their weeks.

This practice has reinforced a concrete habit of being grateful in my life. With gratitude and many other traits, we usually wait for them to come to us as a spontaneous feeling in the moment. Yet if we rely on the arrival of a feeling, we may never actualize this trait. However, taking the first step to practice gratitude when we don't feel like it makes it easier to feel grateful in other moments. I can now call myself a grateful person because I have engrained the practice of gratitude into my life to a level consistent enough that it defines me.

› EVERY DECISION CASTS A VOTE

As we work to understand who we are at the core, and align our actions, I want to emphasize the value of repeated action in facing discomfort and challenging our stories. In the last chapter, driving the truck reinforced a new story about me. Every time I drove it, my brain went through the same pattern of forgiving, trusting, and uprooting fear. In this story, I didn't challenge my story by just being grateful once but by building a new pattern in my life. In both these examples, I didn't just challenge my story by changing. I challenged my story by making a new routine.

The beautiful part of this is that even small actions, when done consistently, have the power to shape who we become. In his book, *Atomic Habits*, James Clear says,

"Every action you take is a vote for the type of person you wish to become. No single instance will transform your beliefs, but as the votes build up, so does the evidence of your new identity. This is one reason why meaningful change does not require radical change. Small habits can make a meaningful difference by providing evidence of a new identity. And if a change is meaningful, it is actually big. That's the paradox of making small improvements." In this way, the effectiveness of a change is measured more by its consistency than by its volume.

> I didn't just challenge my story by changing. I challenged my story by making a new routine.

I want to offer this as an encouragement as you face your fight. What small changes will redirect your trajectory?

- Setting screen time limits
- Writing for fifteen minutes each morning
- Going to bed thirty minutes earlier
- Work out for ten minutes a day
- Joining a community group once a week
- Calling your sibling for ten minutes on your way home from work every Monday
- Giving away $10 to a stranger each month

It's easier to establish routines like this in young adulthood. By the time you get older, it's harder to shift. The small choices you make now cast votes for the person you will be ten years from now.

ACTION PLAN:
UPGRADE YOUR HABITS

Who are you?

1. What are five core things that define who you are? (What are things you care about, roles you're responsible for, and your strengths?)

What are you doing?

2. What five things do you spend the most time on in this season of life?

Why are you doing it?

3. Do those things you're doing align with who you are and want to become?

If your answer is yes, you're in alignment. If your answer is no, consider these questions:

4. What makes you feel alive? List memories, activities, and experiences.
5. What's one+ thing(s) you want to spend more time on to align with this identity?

6. What's one+ thing(s) you want to spend less time on to align with this identity?

7. How can you make these changes into a habit or routine?

8. Who can do this with you or keep you accountable for doing them?

STRATEGY FIVE:

CONSTRUCT YOUR FUTURE

CONSTRUCT YOUR FUTURE

15

THE DIFFERENCE BETWEEN POTENTIAL AND PURPOSE

You are just as worthy, deserving, and capable of creating and sustaining extraordinary health, wealth, happiness, love, and success in your life as any other person on earth. It is absolutely crucial—not only for the quality of your life but for the impact you make on your family, friends, clients, co-workers, children, community, and anyone whose life you touch—that you start living in alignment with that truth.

—HAL ELROD, MIRACLE MORNING

On July 1st, 2013, Diana and I celebrated the opening of Reason Fitness, our gym. I was a twenty-five-year-old kid with a dream and a bank account dropping dollars by the day. I couldn't believe I finessed the leasing agent into signing an agreement. Uncharacteristically, I also reached out for help among the more extensive network of CrossFit gym founders. And one day, it finally happened.

I stood there looking out across this barren cement room, a lone refrigerator lingering in the center from the last tenants—two keys in my hand. Over the next several months, the empty cement room grew full of equipment and machines.

I always say that the gym was my first child because it really felt that way. Building it has been one of the most demanding things I've ever done, especially in the early years. I took a risk on it, and I invested everything I had. In return, it took on a life of its own and grew beyond what I could have hoped.

I could have taken plenty of other perfectly acceptable routes—and still could! It would not have been unacceptable or irresponsible for me to stay in real estate. Building my 401k, I could have saved up for the Mercedes. I might have focused on physical therapy and joined someone else's practice rather than starting a gym. I could have continued coaching clients privately. Other options existed. In many ways, these options would have been more comfortable.

Maybe you can relate. I know many young men who prepared for a career they later weren't so sure was a fit. Some went to college and got a degree. Sometimes, the degree points to a specific career path, but often, it's open-ended. Even if it points to a particular career path, many graduate and find they don't want to pursue the career they thought they did. I also know many who went straight into a trade, so they have some experience under their belt but don't know where to go from there. Perhaps you're interested in doing relief work, playing music, or running a side hustle selling custom dog leashes. Maybe your whole family works in finance. How do you choose how to position yourself for your future? Do you go with your degree? Your experience? Your side hustle? Your passion? The family business? Something risky? Something secure? Go back to school? There are so many options!

Of all the options available to me, there's one reason I feel confident that I found my unique purpose in the world. From my early years to this day, my mom calls me at least once a week. She asks how I'm doing and how her grandkids are, and she tells me about her work and her friends. But she always asks me the same question before we hang up: "Eric, do you still love what you're doing?" And no matter how many hours I worked that week, no matter how much sleep I lost over worrying, even when I wasn't making a penny, my answer was and is always, "Yes." I have fought through an enormous amount of discomfort to win this.

This question has always grounded me. In many ways, the work is much tougher than what I did before. But even when my energy is drained, my cup is full. I am actively living out the reason I was placed on this earth. That feeling is irreplaceable. Even as my purpose evolves, this feeling attests to the fight I have won.

➤ THE SEARCH FOR PURPOSE

I don't know what you're asking, sensing, planning, or pursuing when it comes to your purpose this season. I do know that our twenties and thirties perhaps prompt us to think about our purpose more than ever. Recent data shows that seventy-five percent of young adults have experienced a quarter-life crisis. The most common reasons include career uncertainty, insufficient earnings, inability to buy a house, feeling "stuck in a rut," not enough travel, pressure to get married and/or have kids, and not having achieved personal goals. [16] Few seem to escape this resounding moment of panic.

I'm well-experienced with quarter-life crises. I had a great one myself (my meltdown over not being able to watch *Zero Dark 30*). Besides that, I've been present for quarter-life crises of many of the young men and women I've coached over the last fifteen years. This season, you face weighty questions and trajectory-setting decisions, on top of the discomfort of being in a brand-new season of life. What's clear is that locating our purpose in the transition from adolescence into adulthood is not easy.

Growing up, so much of life is structured for us. Now, we have more autonomy and opportunity than we've ever had before:

> You choose how to spend your time.
> You choose who you spend time with.
> You choose your activities.
> You choose how to spend your money.
> You choose what to study.
> You choose what you want to do for a living.

Where do we go from here? The questions we ask ourselves in this season set the foundation for our lives in the years ahead, making them so terrifying. We are actively forming not just what we will do in the upcoming years, but who we will be as adults in the world. Like building a house, the decisions of young adulthood are the framework—what rooms to include, the layout, and the infrastructure to build on. The last thing we want is to start building, tear it all down, and start over. We long to do it right the first time. But how? There is no blueprint.

This blank canvas is the most thrilling and terrorizing part of this shift. For this reason, a particular paradigm for the understanding of purpose has stuck with me over the years.

› POTENTIAL AND PURPOSE

Potential is a lightbulb, but purpose is a laser. Here's what I mean by that:

When you turn on the lightbulb, light fills the room. It represents all the potential degrees you could get and all the career paths available to you with the education, experiences, and talents you have or could acquire. Also, all the places you could live, all the causes you could give your life to, and all the ways you could spend your time. The voice of opportunity whispers, "You can be *anything*."

Potential is a great thing. Our parents sacrificed for us to have a better childhood than they did, get a good education, and have vast life experiences. We sacrifice for our children, trying to give them opportunities we didn't have. Perhaps we strove to provide ourselves with these opportunities, taking classes and traveling, expanding the horizons of what we could be. The more we learn, experience, and develop a growth mindset, the more opportunities are available. Our lightbulb of potential shines brighter, casting light on more possible paths.

Yet the point of it is not to keep building potential forever. Rather, everything we've experienced and learned leads to deciding what we want to do with it because potential is all about what could happen. The terrifying moment is when we have to decide what will happen. And we start feeling the pressure to figure this out as early as middle and high school. It can be nearly unbearable by the time we graduate college. Rather than taking the first stepping stone in our career, we get a part-time job at Starbucks. Or, in my case, a 24-Hour Fitness. And we look out at all the potential paths we could take, paralyzed in fear of choosing the wrong direction.

Therefore, while potential is a lightbulb, purpose is a laser beam. Potential shows us all we could do; purpose points to the one thing we're meant to do.

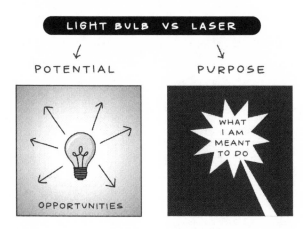

LIGHT BULB VS LASER

POTENTIAL

OPPORTUNITIES

PURPOSE

WHAT I AM MEANT TO DO

Plenty of others will try and impose a purpose onto your life for you. For example, suppose you come from an immigrant family like mine. In that case, they look at your life and choices through the lens of all they've sacrificed to get you here—to build up that lightbulb of potential. You were their most significant investment. They believe your purpose is to finally "make it"—not just for yourself, but for them too. And they may have a specific idea of how that looks. Sometimes our purpose was "assigned" to us at a young age. All these years, we've conceptualized ourselves through that lens, which may or may not align with our true purpose.

> Potential shows us all we could do; purpose points to the one thing we're meant to do.

Regardless of the family you came from, it's not easy to live in America without feeling some level of pressure toward the "American Dream"—go to a good school, get a lucrative job, become financially comfortable, get married and have a big wedding, buy a BMW, buy a house in a good neighborhood with lots of trees and a good school district with a nearby park, have two point five kids, upgrade the car, move to the suburbs, remodel the house, and so on. Regardless of what expectations you grew up under, we all must navigate this tension between the prototype laid on us and the purpose awaiting us.

➤ PRINCIPLES OF PURPOSE

1. Our purpose is not the same as our vocation.

It was clear that while I worked in real estate, I was not living into my purpose. Not because real estate was a bad career, but because I was only in it to follow someone else's plan for my life. My action toward my purpose involved a career shift in opening my gym. We can viscerally feel when a job we're doing does not align with our sense of purpose at all. When we're clocking in and out, we feel empty inside, and our head is always somewhere else.

For this reason and many others, it's tempting to confuse purpose and vocation as the same thing. But while they relate to one another, they are not the same. Your vocation can align with your purpose. However, your whole purpose is not defined by your vocation. Your purpose is far more expansive than that. If part of your purpose is to be a leader, teacher, athlete, or healer, you can live out that purpose in so many ways. It doesn't just exist within your vocation but also defines who you are in your friend groups, your family, and your community. Rather than just being about your vocation, it's also about your relationships, health, growth, and who you are in the world around you.

2. The pathway to purpose is not linear.

We often incorrectly imagine that finding our purpose means entering the field we feel called to immediately out of college (or high school). We stick with it, taking the next logical stepping stone on a path that makes sense. However, this is different from how purpose looks too.

Why? Because our purpose requires you to be a certain person to live it out effectively. If your purpose is to be a teacher, teaching requires humility. Perhaps that job you hated wasn't a waste of time or a step in the wrong direction. Maybe it was meant to create humility in you so that when you were given the opportunity to teach, you would do it in a way that meets people where they were rather than talking down to them. What if that rough season of anxiety where you didn't know where you should live or what your book should be about was intended to build empathy in you? Or get you to consider new possibilities you otherwise wouldn't have? Ultimately, your purpose makes use of the inevitable and nonlinear steps along the way. We do not need to fear them.

3. Our purpose can and will evolve over time.

For a long time, I found so much of my sense of purpose in coaching people one-on-one and in teaching all the classes myself. I have always loved coaching and teaching classes. However, over time, it began to feel like there was something more I should be doing. My laser beam was not shifting direction but was casting its light further, showing me an extension of what I was already doing. It was then that I began "multiplying myself." I saw other young men and women in my gym community whose purpose fit with mine; we complemented each other. I invested less energy in one-on-one coaching and teaching classes and more vigor into mentoring them. Rather than taking away from my purpose, this allowed my purpose to go further than I as an individual could take it, and it allowed me to help others live into their purpose.

If you feel unsatisfied by something that used to make you feel highly purposeful, perhaps your purpose is evolving. Maybe it's time to express your purpose in a new way or at a new level. It may be time to articulate how you envisioned your purpose before and how you see it now.

4. Finding purpose requires our action.

We also think that our purpose can find us with no action on our part. There is a kernel of truth to this. That kernel is that our natural likes, dislikes, passions, and talents often point to our purpose. We didn't necessarily choose these; we may have found them accidentally or observed them over time.

However, for the most part, we find our purpose by pairing our nature with trial and error. How will we know if something lights us up inside if we don't try it? How will we know if we're gifted mentors if we never mentor? How do we determine if we're meant to be teachers if we never try teaching? When we test something, it will either resonate inside us or not. Or maybe that resonance will build over time. Regardless, taking action and trying things we're not used to can help clarify our purpose more quickly and precisely than if we wait and see.

How do we identify the laser of purpose? We identify our purpose by understanding who we are. We must do this in a deep, continuous, and evolving exploration of ourselves and our stories.

As discussed in the last chapter, who are you beneath what you do? What stories about yourself did you challenge? What new stories are you writing for yourself? What are your strengths and passions? Knowing who you are reveals the laser beam that clearly and ruthlessly cuts through all the other noise and shows you exactly where to go.

16

YOUR PURPOSE GROWS WITH YOU

"Our greatest fear in life should not be of failure but of succeeding at things that don't really matter."
—FRANCIS CHAN

When I first started in the fitness industry, I coached clients one-on-one out of a garage—an homage to my parents' business beginnings and a necessity. It filled me up to the brim. I felt alert, content, and purposeful. Yet, over time, I felt like there was something more.

When I opened my gym, I found myself in another "flow state" that lasted for several months. My energy was boundless. I locked my brain in at full capacity, alert and ready to take on any challenge. I knew I was living into my laser-focused purpose. Every day I showed up to work energized. Every class I taught, every client I coached, and every conversation reverberated with this feeling that

I was precisely where I was supposed to be. And yet, in time, it seemed something was missing.

I began building my gym from a one-man band into a community. I stopped teaching every class and coaching every client, and I began investing in others who had extraordinary talent in those areas. I was spending more of my time investing in the development of other leaders at Reason Fitness than trying to lead it all myself. My soul was ablaze as I watched my coaches take on new challenges, discover new strengths, and build our community. I could never have accomplished it alone. I knew this was exactly where I was supposed to be and what I was meant to be doing. And yet, as time went on, I felt that there should be more.

I shared more on podcasts through conversations with others in my industry and community. I started writing more. I joined a Mastermind community to learn more. One of my closest friends and I started a men's community called We The Trust. Not to mention, I began exploring the idea of writing a book.

You may look at this progression and think, "Eric is never satisfied." However, my progression illustrates this truth: our purpose grows as we do. It is not static—it is ever-evolving. And if we follow it, it's always teaching us new things.

In each of these seasons, I never strayed from who I was: a follower, a leader, an athlete, and a lover. But in each season, my purpose manifested differently. The lessons I learned in each season built on one another as long as I was willing to keep taking the next step. This is the process by which we construct our future.

➤ IS THIS WHERE I'M SUPPOSED TO BE?

The shift in each of my seasons started with a feeling that something was missing. I talk with many men who feel that something is missing in their lives. Many feel stuck in their jobs and aimless or dissatisfied with where their lives are right now. Here are a few examples of how this might look outside my life. These are three composites of young men with whom I've worked.

JARED

Our first man is named Jared. Jared's family didn't have much money growing up, and he promised himself that once he was on his own, he wouldn't live a life of financial insecurity. From an early age, he knew that he was good with money and numbers and wanted to go into a job related to finance. He imagined helping other people with his talent. He studied hard in high school and college, then applied to jobs that gleamed with an aura of success. He landed a career as an accountant in a top-tier financial business and continued to work hard.

He's been successful, but his achievements don't give him the satisfaction he thought he'd experience. He'd imagined himself helping people reach their goals, and his current position doesn't give him much chance to work with people. Instead, Jared spends most of his time alone in his office, and there's not much connection among his fellow accountants. It seemed like taking this position was the right choice at the time. But now in his mid-twenties, he feels stuck. Did Jared make a mistake?

ANDRE

Then there's Andre. He works for a small design company doing graphic design for corporate marketing accounts. It's decent money; at first, he enjoyed this work. But he has no say about which clients he's assigned. Andre finds himself daydreaming about going out on his own and being able to pick his clients. He'd like to work with non-profits as well as for-profit businesses. What is the point of going to work every day if your job is monotonous and unrewarding?

Andre feels a similar dissatisfaction in other areas of his life. He's in a committed dating relationship, but it feels stagnant. He hasn't had a community of close friends since high school and is too busy to create a new community. He wonders why he still feels a sense of emptiness even when it seems he has it all together. Why has his life turned out to be so unfulfilling?

CARLOS

Finally, there's Carlos, an only child of parents who worked day and night at their small dry cleaners to give him everything they could. He lacked for nothing and grew up feeling a little self-conscious about it. His family assumed that Carlos would take over the business, so he did. Now he feels like he has no other option but to continue running the business, ensuring that his parents are well cared for as they grow older.

He wonders if following in his parent's footsteps is suitable for him. He loves them deeply, but this pressure he feels stirs conflict with them. Whenever he imagines returning to school or starting a new path, he stops himself. It feels irresponsible to spend the money or lose his and his parents' investment in the family business. Is it too late for him to find a different way?

I believe none of these men "made mistakes" but most likely made the best decisions they could at the time. But one thing I'm sure of is this: it's never too late to re-examine whether you are living according to your life purpose.

➤ PURSUING A DYNAMIC PURPOSE

At these junctures, it's easy to feel like we've made a mistake, wasted our time, and are now stuck. It can be hard to locate our purpose or any road to get there.

> It's never too late to re-examine whether you are living according to your life purpose.

However, there is still a road back. Your purpose is not lost. I believe it is just evolving.

We have the opportunity to follow our evolving purpose if we harness one key skill: having a growth mindset. A growth mindset means you are looking at every job, experience, and person as a teacher. You put every experience to use, gaining insight, knowledge, and expertise toward your purpose. When I started building my gym, I saw how all my prior experiences—even those I deemed insignificant—had prepared me for unexpected parts of my purpose.

A growth mindset is what allows us not to get stuck when our purpose shifts and we haven't entirely relocated it. In these moments, we don't need to panic. Instead, we need to see learning opportunities surrounding us— opportunities to gain insight, wisdom, and understanding. While it's easy to live on autopilot, being a constant learner both expands our opportunities and sharpens our laser beam of purpose.

Previously, I feared I'd made a mistake spending the time I did in real estate. Did the misery I felt after those three years mean I wasted all that time? I felt a lot like these men did. I didn't even want to ask myself the question! It was uncomfortable to wonder if I had wasted my time and potential, and I imagined doing something different and setting out alone.

Yet looking back on it, I see that while being in real estate wasn't ultimately my purpose, I would never call it time wasted. Yes, I was running from the deeper questions in me and choosing the comfortable route that lives into others' expectations. However, I was still able to gain an enormous amount of knowledge and experience working with people in that career that eventually contributed to building my purpose.

When I stopped panicking and began looking at my history with a growth mindset, I could see how even my experience in real estate contributed vital elements to my purpose. Through the three years I worked there, I learned how to run a business from the inside out. I learned how to fire someone. I became versed in how to mop the floors. I began to understand how important it was to make sure coffee was restocked regularly. I ensured the bathrooms had enough toilet paper. I gained experience in accounting for office funds. I learned how to create a culture. And I realized that if I didn't like the culture, I had a say in pushing toward a better one. My purpose would have grown stagnant if I had kept that job because it was time to move on. But the places I had gone before still served me because I was willing to learn from them. In this way, I believe our purpose is very forgiving. Even if we are not initially pursuing it, it has a way of taking our experiences and putting what seems like scraps to use.

This opportunity is available to the men I described, and the same is available to you as you reflect on where you have been and are going. What can you garner even from the experiences, jobs, people, or seasons that seemed draining or aimless? What nuggets of gold hide there? You may only fully know once the next season reveals what tools you need and you discover you have a couple of them! When we continue to ask questions and have a growth mindset, we can track our purpose as it reveals itself, prepares us, and evolves.

If you are in a life season where you feel stuck toward your future, you've most likely outgrown your past decisions. They were probably the best decisions you could make at the time, and this path took you forward. But rather than shame ourselves or feel guilty about where we are now, it's essential to acknowledge that no matter what is in the past, it's time for a self-assessment. Stop and ask yourself this: "Who is writing my story?" If your answer is "my parents," "my partner," or anyone else—if you're not actively shaping your narrative—then it's time to re-evaluate your purpose and your future.

Our purpose does not always evolve in a clear, linear path. Still, it will continue teaching us if we trust and follow it. An evolving purpose may look like a slight shift for some people. For example, you are applying for a new position in the same company or volunteering for something that uses your talents in new ways. It may be time to set new habits in your life, to spend your time differently, or to spend time with other people. It may mean starting a workout routine or journaling each morning.

> Stop and ask yourself this: "Who is writing my story?"

On the other side of the spectrum are those who may need a wholesale change. It could mean leaving your job or going back to school. Conversely, it could mean leaving school and going back to work. Perhaps it's getting out of a relationship or saying yes to a new healthy one. Maybe it means resigning as a school teacher and starting your own business or resigning from your job and becoming a school teacher.

Often, this evolution creates a nerve-wracking moment of confusion. It's when you realize there is something more, but you haven't quite figured out what it is yet. While this redefining moment may feel scary, it is both temporary and necessary. The discomfort does not indicate that your purpose is gone; it means your purpose is growing. Lean into it.

17

THE TRIUMPH OF A NEW TRAJECTORY

Everything can be taken from a man but one thing: the last of the human freedoms—to choose one's attitude in any given set of circumstances, to choose one's own way. When we are no longer able to change a situation, we are challenged to change ourselves.

—VIKTOR FRANKL

Months after my dad gave me the truck, Diana and I met for dinner with a group of families at someone's home. We opened the door and watched as a dozen kids of different ages darted down the hall. We had been coming for a few months now and were starting to get more comfortable. My friend Ryan handed us paper plates and led us to the kitchen.

As the night went on, the men and women wandered into their own groups. I sat in this circle surrounded by other men. Somehow, we ended up talking about our family traditions. Ryan sat next to me and started telling us his. "A few times a year, all the men in my family get in a circle together, like how we are right now," he said. "We go one by one and say something we appreciate about the last generation. About the good they've done and what we're grateful for. The kids for the dads, and the dads for the grandfathers."

People continued talking and moving around me, but my world froze. *Are you kidding me?* I could not wrap my mind around the scene he had described. I couldn't focus on anything else for the rest of the night. I just kept coming back to that image: all these guys— kids, dads, and grandpas—going around and honoring one another. I'd love to say I was happy for them, but I wasn't. I felt so angry. I was overwhelmed by the jealousy in my heart.

Once again, I still felt this hole. Even after my dad bought me the truck, we didn't talk much. When I heard Ryan's story, that hole grew ten times the size. Ryan's story gave me an even bigger vision of what family could be—a more detailed image of what I was missing out on. The ache in me felt unbearable. Why? Why was that? Something in me was longing for more.

It became my turn. Faces around me looked for me to share my family tradition. But my mind was stuck. Instead of giving my answer, I faced Ryan.

"Man, I've been so distracted since you shared your tradition. I'm jealous, and I covet what your family has."

Another uncomfortable thought closely followed. It felt so foreign that I couldn't believe it had come from my own brain. I tried forming it into words as it played out in my brain.

"I just have this feeling that I need to call my dad and tell him I love him. I-I haven't even told him he's going to be a grandfather."

I was still getting to know these men, and it felt so strange to talk to them about my family. But to my surprise, the other men all began nodding and encouraging me, telling me I should do it. Something about letting these other men into my life, with their affirmations and camaraderie, caused a weight to lift from my chest.

"I think you should call him," Ryan said, punctuating the group sentiment.

"Okay. If I still have this feeling tomorrow, I'll do it," I promised.

I said I didn't want to call him just because I was in an emotionally charged state—I wanted to wait and make sure it was a good idea. But the truth was, I waited another day because I was afraid it would be awkward. We'd never had a relationship like that before. We didn't say, "I love you." We didn't talk about our relationship or what we felt. It felt vulnerable. I wasn't sure if he'd say it back—or what he'd say if anything. Giving him a space in my heart again meant he could hurt me again—the very thing I'd hardened myself all those years to prevent.

While these fears were valid, living by them was not producing the life I wanted. I was continuing the same actions—or lack of action—and getting the same results. I needed to be willing to face the conversation I was avoiding. If I wanted something to change, I needed to be willing to change it.

› CLAIMING A VICTORY

I waited until the next day—a chilly Friday. I grabbed my keys from the small table by the door but stopped in the doorway. As I looked out at my old car and the new truck on the street, I put my old keys back on the table and grabbed the new truck keys. As I slid into the seat, I noted how nice it was—faux leather seats and a fresh smell. As I pulled onto the freeway heading south, I noticed the smooth but potent engine. And I knew it was now or never.

"Hello?" my dad answered the phone more like a question than a greeting.

"Hey. So, uh, I was at this group last night. Some guys were talking about their family traditions, things they do with the other men in their family." I took a deep breath. "I know that's something we don't have. I know we haven't always had the best relationship, but I felt envious of what they had. And I wanted to tell you that you're going to be a grandfather. Diana and I are having a baby girl, and I want you to be part of her life." I waited for a reply, but it didn't come. I kept going.

"No strings attached. I don't want anything from you. I just want you to know that I'm not holding onto anything from the past; I just want to have a relationship."

The seconds of silence that passed felt like a year. I tried to imagine what his face must look like—was he holding back tears? Was he wrinkling his nose with disgust and disapproval? Was he checking the caller ID to make sure it was me? I pictured him hunched over, with one calloused hand on his head, pressing dark gray hair from his face.

Then, I heard, "Yes." Just one word.

"Okay. I love you, dad." I ended the call.

I felt like I'd jumped off a high cliff into the water. The adrenaline and shock of the leap led to the calm stillness of the deep water. I wondered, "Did that just happen?" My heart swelled with both disbelief and hope, and I tried to fathom how the moment felt so small and big at the same time.

It felt completely foreign to speak those words to him—like it was another language we were learning. My grandpa had never told my dad he loved him, and my dad had never said it to my grandpa. But as he was getting older, I sensed he was looking back on his life. I could tell something in him had softened, and I think he wanted things to change too.

Along with the truck, he had given me an unintentional gift of acceptance. I finally accepted that no strings were attached, and I did not need to earn it. He was just trying to show he still cared about me, even if he did not have the words. I wanted to give him a gift in return—the gift of acceptance, without making him earn it from me.

As I pulled the new truck into our driveway, I felt a seismic shift happening between how my life would have been and how it could be. This conversation didn't fix everything or erase the past. We didn't suddenly become the family of my dreams—no big expectations, family trips, or holiday arrangements. We just agreed he'd be part of our lives, and that was that. I started driving the truck more as an act of faith. It was a concrete action I could use to practice accepting help despite my pride, receiving love despite our history, and welcoming change despite its discomfort. Though the call was a small act, I knew I'd just won something big.

➤ THE PRIZE THAT AWAITS US

Since that day, my relationship with my dad has continued to grow. We talk more often, he sometimes joins us for dinner, and my children know their grandfather. I have learned more about him in the last few years than I have known about him in my entire life up until this point. Our relationship isn't perfect by any means, but we are in a much different place than where we started.

I share this as the last story of this book because it is one of the most fantastic examples of winning the fight in my experience. My relationship with my father started out as the ultimate wound of my life—the wound that shaped me in far-reaching ways and made me feel trapped for years. That wound threatened to define my life in a way that would cause me to repeat the same sad cycle. Facing this wound has been one of the most uncomfortable journeys of my life. But through facing my fight—and all the discomfort wrapped up in it at every turn—I have gained more growth, wholeness, and freedom than I ever could have imagined as a child.

When I confronted my dad on the doorstep that day at fifteen years old, my victory was hollow. But the feeling that wells inside my chest now is exactly what I expected winning to feel like and more. And I was not the only one who won; my victory meant my dad won too. Fighting the wrong battles all those years only led to win-lose situations. When I finally fought the *right* battles, it created a win-win situation that healed my heart so profoundly that it trickled wholeness into the rest of my life as well.

Fighting the right fight in my life meant that my greatest pains became my most unrivaled victories. Early on, I committed to winning by acknowledging my dissatisfaction and deciding that getting to the root of it was worth the discomfort. Then, I claimed my power when I began to take ownership of my emotions and how my experiences shaped me. I chose to connect, which gave me critical support, vision, and

> Fighting the wrong battles all those years only led to win-lose situations. When I finally fought the *right* battles, it created a win-win situation that healed my heart so profoundly that it trickled wholeness into the rest of my life as well.

accountability for where I wanted to go. And I challenged my story by developing a new sense of who I was. I made decisions based on that rather than simply what I had done in the past. Lastly, I constructed the future I dreamed of by pressing through discomfort to live out my purpose. I continue doing so to this day.

That prize awaits us on the other side of discomfort, a life we always thought was reserved for someone else. It's ours to win and our opportunity to write history.

› ENCOURAGEMENT

I hope this journey through the Freedom Framework together has helped you clarify what fight stands in the way of becoming the man you were meant to be. You can commit to winning by taking stock of what fight lies before you and committing to win. Claim your power over the external and internal forces that have stuck you in cycles of frustration and emptiness. By humbling yourself, you can now lean on the men and women in your life for strength and accountability. Challenge the story you were given and those you've believed about yourself. In constructing your future, do not follow everyone. But do follow your unique purpose wherever it takes you.

This season of life is full of unknowns, and I do not have the answers to the questions that batter your mind as you fall asleep at night. I don't know if your business will make it. I don't know what you'll do down the road or whether you'll be with someone. I don't know where you'll live or if you'll reconcile with your family. I don't know your path ahead. But I am placing my hand on your shoulder and passing these words on to you: *I know you will make it.*

ACTION PLAN:
WRITE YOUR NEW STORY

1. What is one story about yourself you challenged through reading this book?
2. From where did this story come?
3. How has believing this story influenced your life?
4. Why do you need to challenge this story?
5. What discomfort do you need to face?
6. What new story do you want to write?

CONTINUING THE CONVERSATION

This book has come to an end, but this is not the end of the conversation. I'm in your corner. If this book has helped you find any healing, momentum, or clarity in your story, I'd love to connect with you and continue equipping you to be the man you were meant to be. On my website, ericfreedom. com, you'll find more resources and practices for improving habits, health, and the areas of our life that matter most.

I love to connect with like-minded people, and I find it an honor to hear from those who have read my book, listened to me on a podcast, or attended one of my speaking engagements. If you have questions or want to say hi, find me on social media @coachericfreedom or click the Connect tab on my website to send me a message. I would love to add as much value to your journey as possible, and I look forward to hearing from you.

AFTERWORD

Earlier this year, my five-year-old daughter Harper wanted to learn how to ride a bike. Riding always hurt my butt, but I was excited to help her explore something new. Besides, it was starting to get warmer, but the extreme summer heat hadn't kicked in yet. We went to a local bike shop and picked out a bike for her—a pink one with yellow flowers and a basket.

She started with training wheels but couldn't get them off fast enough. Then Harper set her sights on going down a ten-foot hill. It was this big hill at the park near our house. As she played on the swings and bars, she watched with wide eyes as the older kids bombed down it. They flew across the black asphalt slope like a flock of birds, effortlessly coasting in victory. She practiced and practiced—keeping her balance, going through dips, moving on and off the grass. She rehearsed up and down a ten-foot driveway in preparation. Once she'd mastered it, she knew she was ready for the hill.

We tossed her bike in the car and drove over, perching her bike at the top of the steep slope. It looked even steeper from the top, and its size seemed to dwarf my daughter, even with her larger-than-life confidence. But I couldn't have stopped her if I had tried. Before I knew it, she was in motion, like a rollercoaster inching over the edge to the drop. I held my breath.

Time moved at a snail's pace as I watched her. She was a quarter of the way and doing well. She was halfway, and her bike was steering to the side.

"Straighten it out, Harper!" I yelled.

She was three-quarters the way there and heading toward some uneven pavement on the far side of the hill.

"Harper!" I shouted, but it made no difference.

Before I knew it, she hit the uneven pavement, her wheel twisted, and she lost control. The bike fell sideways, and she tumbled off of it.

Everything else around me blurred as I sprinted down the hill to her. "Harper, Harper, are you okay? Where did you hit?"

She slowly sat up as I rapidly checked her for cuts and contusions. As she looked up at me, I saw her nose bleeding. She didn't cry, and she said she was okay, but I carried her back up to the top. I set her down on the grass and cleaned up her nose and a few other scrapes on her legs.

"You ready to go home? Let's go get some lunch."

To my surprise, she shook her head. She looked at me and asked, "Can I go again?"

I was in shock. "Harper, you just wiped out down there. You want to go again right now?"

She nodded. "I know what happened. When I started going really fast, I forgot to steer. I went too far from the side. But the other kids all stayed in the middle. I know what to do now."

As we end our journey through this book, I want to leave you with this story of my daughter as an encouragement.

Harper did not start out knowing how to ride a bike. Riding a bike is not something she's often seen me do either. Every next step she took on that bike was uncharted territory. And yet with every small new accomplishment, she charted the territory for herself. And each time, she set a precedent that gave her more confidence she could face the next challenge—from training wheels to two wheels, from a ten-foot driveway to a ten-foot hill. She did not shame herself for not knowing what to do or making a mistake. She was learning something for the first time. Rather than getting bogged down in fear, she perceived her successes and failures as data to help her figure out how to reach her goal.

As you face your fight and continue growing, long after you've read this book, you will find yourself up against hills that feel big and scary that you have never set foot on before. By the nature of rewriting your story, you will tread places no one in your family has ever gone. You will leave the beaten path and find yourself in uncharted territory.

When you get to the top, you may have a moment of panic. You may lose all confidence that this is a fight you can win. Your inner critic will rage at you, telling you that you should know what you're doing.

I want to encourage you with this: the fact that you don't yet know what you're doing is a sign that you are treading in new territory. That is evidence of your growth. That is a testament that you have left your comfort zone for the sake of constructing a new future. You should feel so proud of yourself. Give yourself the grace you'd give a child learning how to ride a bike for the first time. Capture that zeal. Release the need to get it right.

The confidence? That comes later. Of course, you don't have confidence right now! You've never done this before. Confidence is not a given—you must earn it. Like my daughter, you gain confidence by taking one small step after the other. Harper earned confidence through her reps. Through this process, you will do the same.

Your small steps of courage will build a history of failure and success that eventually enables you to do something you never dreamed you could do. So keep taking small steps. Keep casting votes for the person you want to become. Fight the good fight. Lastly, as my life mantra goes: *"Let's gooooooooooooooo!"*

> The fact that you don't yet know what you're doing is a sign that you are treading in new territory. That is evidence of your growth. That is a testament that you have left your comfort zone for the sake of constructing a new future.

ACKNOWLEDGMENTS

Writing an acknowledgment is almost as difficult as writing a book.

It has taken more than two years to complete this book. If this publication was a finish line, the number of people who have helped me cross it is countless. Even beyond that, this book was born of my own story. Countless people add words to the stories that become our lives. So I know I'm going to forget someone here who does not deserve to be forgotten. If you are that person, my deepest apologies.

Few have shaped my story as much as my wife. Diana, where do I begin? Lucky? Do I believe in luck? I'm not sure, but whenever I reflect on our relationship, I feel like the luckiest man alive. You held me tall when I felt I was at rock bottom. There is no one else I'd want by my side, storming in to fight the battles to come. You inspire me to live a more purposeful life worth fighting for.

Mom, growing up, I used to say that the strength of my single mother accounted for the power of two parents. Despite all you've gone through, you made me feel this way. I am proud to be your son. You have always been my biggest fan and supporter. You've instilled in me a confidence that most people never harness in their entire lifetime. Your willpower, strength, and commitment to raising me and Patrick is something I will never be able to explain to another human being fully. I love you, Mom.

Dad, this was a difficult book for me to write. I've never wholly been able to explain or understand the complexity of our relationship up to this point. This book has helped me process nearly our entire relationship and what it means to be a son. I'm so grateful for the time we have together these days. I am thankful that it was not too late. I think of what you told me about Ye Ye before he passed, and every day I'm reminded of the impermanence of life on earth. If we are lucky, we might get eighty years, fifty of them shared with our parents. Thank you for the lessons I've learned, even the ones taught inadvertently. I love you, Dad.

Patrick, it is a gift to be your brother. You were the first person I ever taught. The first person I ever led. What a life we have lived. Love you, baby brother.

I want to thank the friends who have fought by my side and formed me over the years: Caleb Lin, Ibzan Vidaurre, Kenneth Ren, Mike Whang, Peter Lin, Phillip Chan, Philip Tseng, Steve Lee, and Thomas Wong. Thank you for your friendship. I'm grateful for how it has formed me over the years.

I also want to thank the men who have led, mentored, and shaped me: Chris Chu, Chris Cooper, Daniel Wong,

Donald Kong, Erwin Regidor, Guido Trinidad, John Lo, Kenny Wong, Mario Quezada, Morris Li, Paul Tran, Roger Lam, Scott Yang, Terrence Shay, Thomas Wu. Your wisdom bursts from these pages just as much as my own.

Thank you to my team at Reason for holding down the fort for two years so I could complete this project. Reason was my first child—you all are my family.

To the Berry Powell Press team, wow. We did it. We made it. Carmen, thank you for speaking over me that I was an author long before I even thought I could write. This book exists because you saw something in me before I could see it for myself. Abby, we're bonded forever through this project. Without this team, this message would not be what it is. Thank you to Carolyn Rafferty, Valeri Mills Barnes, Marianne Croonquist, Kathleen Taylor, Nico Chera, James Whitfield, Kay McConnaughey, and Jazmin Welch for your creativity and insight. Each of you has helped me give the world a message it needs to hear. Let's change the world.

APPENDIX

HEALTH IN ONE HUNDRED WORDS

One of my missions is to help people live happier, healthier lives. There is an undeniable, innate connection between those two goals. Greater internal clarity often shows us how valuable it is to steward our bodies. Investing in our physical bodies bolsters our inner strength and clarity. That's why I wanted to take a moment at the end of this book to address our physical health more specifically.

I could talk about the power of our physical health for hours on end—and I have. But here, the one point I want to make is this: depending on how we steward it, our physical health can either be our ceiling or our gateway. It can either be an asset or a liability toward our goals. When we invest in our bodies, our actions concretely affirm our self-worth on an existential level. Your choices say, "I'm an important person to take care of." Declaring this truth through our actions pushes the needle toward believing it's true. Then, when we try to reach our goals in other areas of our life, we do so with a greater belief that we are worthy. We're more capable of expanding our limits. We know we can overcome challenges because we have a measurable precedent. We sleep better, have more energy, get injured less easily, and get sick less frequently. All this expands our capacity for what we are both physically and mentally able to shoulder as we pursue our growing purpose.

I share plenty on this topic on my website, blog posts, podcasts, and social media, including recipes, health tips for busy people and professionals, habit trackers, etc. I encourage you to explore those if you're interested.

For now, I want to leave you with my definition of health. At a conference, I was tasked with summarizing it in one hundred words. So, below you'll find what health means to me. You'll notice it's not just about fitness and nutrition. It blends the physical aspects of health with the mental, emotional, and relational tenets we've journeyed through in this book.

My definition of health in one hundred words:

Create an environment where you eat well, move often, think deeply, connect meaningfully, and prioritize rest. Pursue vitality of life with longevity. Combine hope with intention and action. Relentlessly seek what makes you come alive. Control your breathing. Experience nature. Protect your attention. Desire discomfort and challenge yourself with situations that grow you. Listen and reflect. Audit your relationship circle. Serve something bigger than yourself. Create a buffer and margin against sickness. Focus on what you can control, and let go of what you can't. Prefer consistency and sustainability over immediate results. Give yourself love and grace because you matter.

I encourage you to think about what health means to you and consider ways to integrate more movement and better nutrition into your life on a daily and weekly basis. No matter what anyone has told you, what habits you've sustained in the past, or what kind of person you feel you are, your investment in yourself is a vote for your ability, capacity, and confidence.

NOTES

1   Marla Paul, "How Traumatic Memories Hide In The Brain, and How To Retrieve Them," Northwestern Medicine, Feinberg School of Medicine, August 18, 2015, accessed August 5, 2022, https://news.feinberg.northwestern.edu/2015/08/17/how-traumatic-memories-hide-in-the-brain/.

2   "Understanding the conversation gap: Why employees aren't talking, and what we can do about it." Bravely. Accessed August 12, 2022, https://learn.workbravely.com/hubfs/Understanding-the-Conversation-Gap.pdf?t=1533596048056&utm_campaign=smart%20brief%20test&utm_source=hs_automation&utm_medium=email&utm_content=64321921&_hsenc=p2ANqtz-_4k_KzRnQlCrerxB5Gr0XEMMWshlLmigMT3ElhTx6htsOUK3kcp7H-J_GAqZMvIAdILhbkkDX2sEDVSXIQdx9e-xqh8A&_hsmi=64321921.

3   Aaron Smith, "U.S. Smartphone Use in 2015," Pew Research Center, April 1, 2015, accessed August 14, 2022, https://www.pewresearch.org/internet/2015/04/01/us-smartphone-use-in-2015/.

4   "Escape to the movies? 1 in 4 people do: poll," Reuters, March 5, 2010, accessed July 20, 2022, https://www.reuters.com/article/us-movies-poll/escape-to-the-movies-1-in-4-people-do-poll-idustre6243n020100305.

5   Ranganathan, Vinoth K et al. "From mental power to muscle power—gaining strength by using the mind," *Neuropsychologia* 42, no. 7 (2004): 944-56, doi:10.1016/j.neuropsychologia.2003.11.018

6   A.J Adams, "Seeing Is Believing: The Power of Visualization," Psychology Today, December 3, 2009, accessed Aug 5, 2022, https://www.psychologytoday.com/us/blog/flourish/200912/seeing-is-believing-the-power-visualization.

7   Adams, "Seeing Is Believing: The Power of Visualization."

8   Stephanie Pappas, "APA issues first-ever guidelines for practice with men and boys," *Monitor on Psychology*, 50, no. 1 (2019): accessed Sept 1, 2022, https://www.apa.org/monitor/2019/01/ce-corner.

9   Oxford English Dictionary, "emotional intelligence, n.," Oxford UP, 2015, https://www.oed.com/.

10 National Coalition Against Domestic Violence, "Domestic violence and children," 2015, accessed June 5, 2022, retrieved from 111.ncadv.org.

11 Dr. Gloria Wilcox, "Feelings Wheel," RewardCharts 4Kids, 2022, accessed Nov 15, 2022, https://www.rewardcharts4kids.com/feelings-wheel/.

12 Daniel A. Cox, "Men's Social Circles are Shrinking," Survey Center on American Life, June 29, 2021, accessed

Aug 20, 2022, https://www.americansurveycenter. org/why-mens-social-circles-are-shrinking/.

13 Luisa Dillner, "Is having no social life as bad for you as smoking?," The Guardian, Jan 11, 2016, accessed Sept 5, 2022, https://www.theguardian. com/lifeandstyle/2016/jan/11/is-having-no-social-lif e-as-bad-for-you-as-smoking#:~:text=Studies%20 since%20the%201980s%20have,smoking%20or%20 not%20taking%20exercise.

14 Rebecca Riffkin, "In U.S., 55% of Workers Get Sense of Identity From Their Job," Gallup, August 22, 2014, accessed Sept 11, 2022, https://news.gallup.com/ poll/175400/workers-sense-identity-job.aspx.

15 Stephanie Pappas, "The toll of job loss," Monitor on Psychology, 51, no. 7 (2020): accessed Sept 1, 2022, https://www.apa.org/monitor/2020/10/toll-job-loss.

16 LinkedIn Corporate Communications, "New LinkedIn shows 75 percent of 25—33 year-olds have experienced quarter-life crises," LinkedIn Pressroom, Nov 15, 2017, accessed Sept 12, 2022, https://news. linkedin.com/2017/11/new-linkedin-research-show s-75-percent-of-25-33-year-olds-have-e.

BIBLIOGRAPHY

Adams, A.J. "Seeing Is Believing: The Power of Visualization." Psychology Today. December 3, 2009. Accessed Aug 5, 2022. https://www.psychologytoday.com/us/blog/flourish/200912/seeing-is-believing-the-power-visualization.

Cox, Daniel A. "Men's Social Circles are Shrinking." Survey Center on American Life. June 29, 2021. Accessed Aug 20, 2022. https://www.americansurvey-center.org/why-mens-social-circles-are-shrinking/.

Dillner, Luisa. "Is having no social life as bad for you as smoking?" The Guardian. Jan 11, 2016. Accessed Sept 5, 2022. https://www.theguardian.com/life-andstyle/2016/jan/11/is-having-no-social-life-as-bad-for-you-as-smoking#:~:text=Studies%20since%20the%201980s%20have,smoking%20or%20not%20taking%20exercise.

"Escape to the movies? 1 in 4 people do: poll." Reuters. March 5, 2010. Accessed July 20, 2022. https://www.reuters.

com/article/us-movies-poll/escape-to-the-movies-1-in-4-people-do-poll-idustre6243n020100305.

LinkedIn Corporate Communications. "New LinkedIn shows 75 percent of 25—33-year-olds have experienced quarter-life crises." LinkedIn Pressroom. Nov 15, 2017. Accessed Sept 12, 2022. https://news.linkedin.com/2017/11/new-linkedin-research-shows-75-percent-of-25-33-year-olds-have-e.

National Coalition Against Domestic Violence. "Domestic violence and children." 2015. Accessed June 5, 2022. Retrieved from 111.ncadv.org.

Oxford English Dictionary. "Emotional intelligence, n." Oxford UP, 2015. https://www.oed.com.

Pappas, Stephanie. "APA issues first-ever guidelines for practice with men and boys." *Monitor on Psychology 50*, no. 1 (2019). Accessed Sept 1, 2022. https://www.apa.org/monitor/2019/01/ce-corner.

Pappas, Stephanie. "The toll of job loss." Monitor on Psychology 51, no. 7 (2020). Accessed Sept 1, 2022. https://www.apa.org/monitor/2020/10/toll-job-loss.

Paul, Marla. "How Traumatic Memories Hide In The Brain, and How To Retrieve Them." Northwestern Medicine, Feinberg School of Medicine. August 18, 2015. accessed August 5, 2022. https://news.

feinberg.northwestern.edu/2015/08/17/how-traumatic-memories-hide-in-the-brain/.

Ranganathan, Vinoth K et al. "From mental power to muscle power—gaining strength by using the mind." *Neuropsychologia* 42, no. 7 (2004): 944-56. doi:10.1016/j.neuropsychologia.2003.11.018

Riffkin, Rebecca. "In U.S., 55% of Workers Get Sense of Identity from Their Job." Gallup. August 22, 2014. Accessed Sept 11, 2022. https://news.gallup.com/poll/175400/workers-sense-identity-job.aspx.

Smith, Aaron. "U.S. Smartphone Use in 2015." Pew Research Center. April 1, 2015. Accessed August 14, 2022. https://www.pewresearch.org/internet/2015/04/01/us-smartphone-use-in-2015/.

"Understanding the conversation gap: Why employees aren't talking, and what we can do about it." Bravely. Accessed August 12, 2022. https://learn.workbravely.com/hubfs/Understanding-the-Conversation-Gap.pdf?t=1533596048056&utm_campaign=smart%20brief%20test&utm_source=hs_automation&utm_medium=email&utm_content=64321921&_hsenc=p2ANqtz-_4k_KzRnQlCrerxB5Gr0XEMMWshlLmigMT3ElhTx6htsOUK3kcp7H-J_GAqZMvIAdILhbkkDX2sEDVSXIQdx9e--xqh|8A&_hsmi=64321921.

Wilcox, Gloria. "Feelings Wheel." RewardCharts4Kids. 2022. Accessed Nov 15, 2022. https://www.reward-charts4kids.com/feelings-wheel/.

ABOUT THE AUTHOR

Eric Freedom (Chang) was born and raised in Southern California. Eric is a coach turned author passionate about helping men find purpose in today's confusing and challenging world.

While he attended Biola University to study Kinesiology, Eric started his coaching practice out of his garage. After graduating, Eric struggled in his search for purpose. This resulted in launching his first business, CrossFit Reason, in 2012, which has since grown into a familial community committed to pursuing deep health together.

Eric is now a coach, entrepreneur, author, husband, and father of three. Eric also hosts a podcast, Finding Reason, and is co-founder of a men's community, We the Trust. Eric's faith guides his passion—to help others find their purpose, challenging them to steward their minds, bodies, and spirits well. He lives with his wife and three children in Temple City, California.

To learn more and connect with Eric, visit www.ericfreedom.com.

NOTE FROM THE PUBLISHER

We at Berry Powell Press are committed to cultivating authors and their life-changing messages through a collaborative creative community. To this end, we carefully select the books we publish to ensure they align with our values and purpose. We are proud to have Eric Freedom (Chang) as part of our author family for multiple reasons.

First, Eric embodies his message. Fiercely committed to truth-telling, Eric shares his full story—the painful realities along with the breakthroughs. He writes from a heart of compassion and courage, and his vulnerability invites others to experience freedom.

Second, this book speaks to the very real challenges facing young men in our world. Refusing to accept limiting clichés about what it takes to become a "man," Eric explains how to become a self-aware, emotionally intelligent adult. Rather than measuring success by outward accomplishments, he models it through the quality of his relationships and the impact of the care he lavishes upon everyone who crosses his path.

Finally, Eric traverses social boundaries that often divide us—those of race, culture, gender, and belief systems. His authenticity is disarming and allows his message to unite men of all backgrounds around the common goal of reclaiming their power and purpose.

It's an honor to be able to launch this book into the marketplace. If you have a message that needs to become a book, please visit our website at www.berrypowellpress.com.

Berry Powell Press is a hybrid publishing house that publishes authors with transformational perspectives on timely personal and societal challenges. We provide our authors with in-depth mentorship and collaborative assistance to create life-changing books. Additionally, we assist them in building book-based businesses that can impact the largest audience possible. We publish fiction and non-fiction for adults and children.